Peter Roe

Tolkien and the Gothic

Proceedings of The Tolkien Society
Seminar 2022

Edited by Will Sherwood

Contents

About the Peter Roe Memorial Fund

The Tolkien Society's seminar proceedings and other booklets are typically published under the auspices of the Peter Roe Memorial Fund, a fund in the Society's accounts that commemorates a young member who died in a traffic accident. Peter Roe, a young and very talented person joined the Society in 1979, shortly after his sixteenth birthday. He had discovered Middle-earth some time earlier, and was so inspired by it that he even developed his own system of runes, similar to the Dwarvish Angerthas, but which utilised logical sound values, matching the logical shapes of the runes. Peter was also an accomplished cartographer, and his bedroom was covered with multi-coloured maps of the journeys of the fellowship, plans of Middle-earth, and other drawings.

Peter was also a creative writer in both poetry and prose—the subject being incorporated into his own *Dwarvish Chronicles*. He was so enthusiastic about having joined the Society that he had written a letter ordering all the available back issues, and was on his way to buy envelopes when he was hit by a speeding lorry outside his home.

Sometime later, Jonathan and Lester Simons (at that time Chairman and Membership Secretary respectively) visited Peter's parents to see his room and to look at the work on which he had spent so much care and attention in such a tragically short life. It was obvious that Peter had produced, and would have continued to produce, material of such a high standard as to make a complete booklet, with poetry, calligraphy, stories and cartography. The then committee set up a special account in honour of Peter, with the consent of his parents, which would be the source of finance for the Society's special publications. Over the years a number of members have made generous donations to the fund.

The first publication to be financed by the Peter Roe Memorial Fund was *Some Light on Middle-earth* by Edward Crawford, published in 1985. Subsequent publications have been composed from papers delivered at Tolkien Society workshops and seminars, talks from guest speakers at the Annual Dinner, and collections of the best articles from past issues of *Amon Hen*, the Society's bulletin.

Dwarvish Fragments, an unfinished tale by Peter, was printed in *Mallorn* 15 (September 1980). A standalone collection of Peter's creative endeavours is currently being prepared for publication.

The Peter Roe Series

Abbreviations

A&I	*The Lay of Aotrou and Itroun*, ed. by Verlyn Flieger (London: HarperCollins, 2016)
Arthur	*The Fall of Arthur,* ed. by Christopher Tolkien (London: HarperCollins, 2013; Boston: Houghton Mifflin Harcourt, 2013)
AW	*Ancrene Wisse* (Oxford: Oxford University Press, 1962)
B&L	*Beren and Lúthien*, ed. by Christopher Tolkien (London: HarperCollins, 2017)
Beowulf	*Beowulf: A Translation and Commentary, together with Sellic Spell*, ed. by Christopher Tolkien (London: HarperCollins, 2014; Boston: Houghton Mifflin Harcourt, 2014)
Bombadil	*The Adventures of Tom Bombadil and other verses from the Red Book* (London: George Allen & Unwin, 1962; Boston: Houghton Mifflin, 1962)
CoH	*The Children of Húrin*, ed. by Christopher Tolkien (London: HarperCollins, 2007; Boston: Houghton Mifflin Harcourt, 2007)
Exodus	*The Old English Exodus*, ed. by Joan Turville-Petre (Oxford: Oxford University Press, 1982)
Father Christmas	*Letters from Father Christmas*, ed. by Baillie Tolkien (London: George Allen & Unwin, 1976; Boston: Houghton Mifflin, 1976)

Monsters	*The Monsters and the Critics and Other Essays* (London: George Allen & Unwin, 1983; Boston: Houghton Mifflin, 1984)
Morgoth	*Morgoth's Ring*, ed. by Christopher Tolkien (London: Geore, 1993; Boston: Houghton Mifflin, 1993)
OFS	*Tolkien On Fairy-stories*, ed. by Verlyn Flieger and Douglas A. Anderson (London: HarperCollins, 2008)
P&S	*Poems and Stories* (London: George Allen & Unwin, 1980; Boston: Houghton Mifflin, 1994)
Peoples	*The Peoples of Middle-earth*, ed. by Christopher Tolkien (London: HarperCollins, 1996; Boston: Houghton Mifflin, 1996)
Perilous Realm	*Tales from the Perilous Realm* (London: HarperCollins, 1997)
RK	*The Return of the King*
Silmarillion	*The Silmarillion*, ed. by Christopher Tolkien (London: George Allen & Unwin, 1977; Boston: Houghton Mifflin, 1977).
Sauron	*Sauron Defeated*, ed. by Christopher Tolkien (London: HarperCollins, 1992; Boston: Houghton Mifflin, 1992)
Secret Vice	*A Secret Vice: Tolkien on Invented Languages*, ed. by Dimitra Fimi and Andrew Higgins (London: HarperCollins, 2016)

Introduction

Will Sherwood

"Gothic was the first [language] to take me by storm, to move my heart. [...] I have since mourned the loss of Gothic literature" (Monster, 191–2)

What did the words 'Goth' and 'Gothic' mean to J.R.R. Tolkien? Although we may naturally associate them with the emerging Gothic architecture, aesthetic, and literature of the eighteenth century, the cultural and linguistic history of the Goths was, perhaps, of more importance and interest to Tolkien. Having been exposed to the remnants of the Gothic language early on through Joseph Wright's *A Primer of the Gothic Language* (1910), he was inspired to expand on the language, creating Gautisk from Gothic's fragments and writing the poem 'Bagmē Blōma' that appeared in *Songs for the Philologists* (1936). The language was further repurposed for the nomenclature of early Rhovanion and the Éothéod, ensuring Gothic's posterity through his own legendarium.[1] Although Tolkien "made a distinction between historically recorded Gothic and his own reconstructed Gothic" (Smith 2006, 269), his consciously repetitive acts of preservation and renewal *through* poetry

---

1. See Christopher Tolkien's note on page 403 of *Unfinished Tales*.

and nomenclature resonates deeply with his own idea that "mythology is language and language is mythology" (*OFS*, 181). Verlyn Flieger unpacks this phrase well, explaining that "to say that language is mythology is to say in essence that encoded *in the words* and indivisible *from the words* are the beliefs and assumptions of the culture, the national soul that undergirds the stories" (2024,128; emphasis original). Conclusively for Tolkien, the 'soul' of the Gothic may have been fragmented, but it had not been completely lost.

There have been various studies of Tolkien's aim to 'replenish' aspects of history and language through his legendarium. His early ambition to provide England with its missing mythology specifically with *The Book of Lost Tales* (1910s-1930s)[2] has perhaps received the most attention. Nick Groom, however, has broadened the scope of the Gothic discussion by positing that Tolkien was part of an ongoing Catholic Gothic tradition that included figures such as Richard Verstegan, Edmund Burke, and Augustus Welby Pugin. *The Lord of the Rings*, Groom suggests, is specifically part of the Puginian Gothic Revival as Pugin's architectural style sought to "revive medieval social structures [...] because they were consistent with his faith, which was itself continuous with the Middle Ages" (2016, 33). Tolkien, Groom notes, similarly grounded his work in the values of medieval Catholicism, implying to a war-torn twentieth century audience how "community relations in a Christian society can be reforged" (34). This leads to the implication that *The Lord of the Rings* houses the tools required to heal a society divided from centuries of religious conflict and two World Wars.

---

2. See Dimitra Fimi's *Tolkien, Race and Cultural History: From Fairies to Hobbits* (2008) which documents the growth of Tolkien's legendarium and ties the Romantic nationalism of his 'mythology for England' with the development and abandonment of *The Book of Lost Tales*.

Of course, it is not a surprise that an author who fought in the Great War, witnessed the lead up to and fallout of World War Two employed Gothic tropes across six decades of writing. Whether a conscious or unconscious influence, Fred Botting's useful summary of what Gothic texts can constitute[3] helps us understand the genre's appeal to Tolkien, whose depictions of war are anything but glorified and Romanticised:

> overtly but ambiguously, not rational, depicting disturbances of sanity and security, from superstitious belief in ghosts and demons, displays of uncontrolled passion, violent emotion or flights of fancy to portrayals of perversion and obsession. (2014, 2)

Reviewing the many tales of Tolkien's legendarium and their many renditions in light of Botting's list leads to the conclusion that Arda is inherently and inextricably Gothic in nature. From Tolkien's use of traditionally Gothic 'supernatural'[4] creatures such as werewolves, ghosts, and hybrids, to the trauma-influenced behaviour and psychology of characters like Elendil, Sméagol/Gollum, and Túrin Turambar, the Gothic aesthetic permeates the legendarium.

Although the Gothic literary tradition began in the eighteenth century as an antithesis to the ideals and philosophies of the Enlightenment, it is critical that we do not overlook that Tolkien experienced the tail-end of the *fin de siècle* when some of the most prolific British Gothic texts were written and

---

3. I use 'can constitue' here as the Gothic is a complex and multifaceted genre that does not conform to simple definitions. Its continuous evolution allows it to move beyond simplifications - as can be seen in the current volume.

4. Tolkien's own thoughts on the word 'supernatural' are not so straightforward. See his comments in 'On Fairy-stories'.

published. Imagine growing up and hearing about the possible duality of human consciousness and the primal fury innate in us all in *The Strange Case of Dr Jekyll and Mr Hyde* (1886), the price of selling your soul to the Devil and eternal youth in *The Picture of Dorian Gray* (1890), the threat of colonialism and the collapse of the British empire in *Dracula* (1897), the unravelling horrors of human behaviour in the *Sherlock Holmes* series (1887-1927). Whether Tolkien read the treasure trove of genre-defining texts published during his formative years or not, it is impossible that he was not aware of them and the controversies surrounding each one, just as audiences were collectively aware of the Barbenheimer phenomenon in 2023.[5] With the colossal outpouring of revolutionary Gothic narratives, it is additionally understandable why Tolkien readily applied the genre's tropes as early as *The Book of Lost Tales*, reflecting his time's literary zeitgeist.

So what did the words 'Goth' and 'Gothic' mean to J.R.R. Tolkien? Aside from the Gothic aesthetic being part of the popular culture of the late nineteenth and early twentieth centuries, the remnants of the Gothic language presented him with the opportunity to continue its legacy into the twentieth century through his poetry and legendarium. Further, the Gothic Revival tied Tolkien to historical figures who also implicitly tried to heal society. The fact that Tolkien was surrounded by advances in the Gothic literary genre further provided the perfect encouragement to utilise and experiment with its ingredients in his own work. The Goths and the Gothic became integral to Tolkien's writing and it can be argued that

---

5. On 21st July, 2023, *Barbie* and *Oppenheimer* were released, leading to one of the highest grossing weekends in cinema history as audiences rose to the challenge of seeing both films back-to-back.

he succeeded in conserving the Gothic as readers of his letters, biographies, and fiction seek to learn more about the people, their culture, and language to this day.

Tolkien and the Gothic was the Tolkien Society's first hybrid seminar, offering in-person and online papers and continuing to welcome speakers from across the globe. Of the eleven papers presented at the seminar, seven are presented in this proceedings. Mahdî Brecq opens this volume by exploring how Tolkien based some of the verses from 'Bagmē blōma' on passages from the Wulfila Bible, and more particularly on what might be called the 'Gothic poetic elements' preserved in the Gothic Bible. Kristine Larsen follows by delving into the Gothic nature of 'The Tale of Adanel' as the original fall, considering its setting in the distant past of a Medievalist world and supernatural atmosphere of mystery and terror among other key elements of the Gothic. Next, the seminar's keynote speaker, Nick Groom, examines how the different peoples of Middle-earth can be considered crypto-Gothic before looking beyond Sigmund Freud's staple Gothic trope of the *unheimlich* ('uncanny') to consider how Tolkien's Middle-earth can be perceived as eldritch: simultaneously familiar and wondrous. Sofia Skeva proceeds by evaluating how the projection of the Gothic monster represents onto the figure of the stranger in Tolkien's literary text propagates an essentialist approach to cultural difference, replicating values linked to imperialist ideologies with both monstrosity and otherness deeply racialized, signifying the 'outsider'. Michael Dunn explores how Tolkien's literary ecology, peoples and monsters, and their languages are uncanny. The penultimate paper by Journee Cotton argues that Saruman's 'genetic' manipulation of bodies 'creates' what may be read as genetically engineered 'designer babies' through an ecoGothic and Environmental Bioethics framework, further considering how Saruman's biotic tinkering appears to coincide with the destruction of Isengard's ecosystem. D.A.K. Watson concludes the proceedings by reading *The Lord of the Rings* through the lens of Tzvetan Todorov's Fantastic, revealing not only how Tolkien achieves the effect of suspense for the reader, but also how its application connects his writing back to the late-Victorian Romances of William Morris, George MacDonald, and H. Rider Haggard.

On behalf of the Tolkien Society, I would like to extend my deepest gratitude to the presenters of the Tolkien Society 2022 Seminar, without whom the event would not have happened. I would also like to thank the Society's committee for their continued support and guidance in the planning and running of the event, and the publishing of this proceedings. The publication itself is made possible by the generosity of the Peter Roe Memorial Fund, for which I am grateful.

Bibliography

Botting, Fred, *Gothic*, 2nd edition, (London: Routledge, 2014).

Flieger, Verlyn, 'Words, Words, Words: Tolkien, Barfield and Romanticism', in *The Romantic Spirit in the Works of J.R.R. Tolkien*, ed. by Will Sherwood and Julian Eilmann (Zurich: Walking Tree Publishers, 2024), pp. 127-146.

Groom, Nick, 'Tolkien and the Gothic', in *The Return of the Ring: Proceedings of the Tolkien Society Conference 2012*, Volume 2, ed. by Lynn Forest-Hill (Edinburgh: Luna Press Publishing, 2016), pp. 25-34.

Smith, Arden. R., 'Tolkienian Gothic', in *The Lord of the Rings 1954 – 2004: Scholarship in Honor of Richard E. Blackwelder*, ed. by Wayne G. Hammond and Christina Scull (Milwaukee: Marquette University Press, 2006) pp. 267-283.

Tolkien, J.R.R., *Tolkien On Fairy-stories*, ed. by Verlyn Flieger and Douglas A. Anderson (London: HarperCollins, 2008).
—, *The Monsters and the Critics and Other Essays*, ed. by Christopher Tolkien (London: HarperCollins, 2006).

Tolkien's Gothic: A Poetic Resurgence?

Mahdî Brecq

In 1936, at University College London, a small collection of songs and poems was published: *Songs for the Philologists* (1936). It was published, as the masthead at the bottom of page four indicates, by "G. Tillotson, A. H. Smith, B. Pattinson and other members of the English Department, University College, London". The collection has the following subtitle: *Mál-rúnar skaltu kunna*, which means "the runes of (the) word you must know" in Old Icelandic. The content of this collection is clear: the place is reserved for the word, that is, by extension, for languages. *Songs for the Philologists* consists of thirty texts in various languages. Thirteen of these texts are attributed to J.R.R. Tolkien. There are eleven texts written in Icelandic, eight in English, six in Old English, two in Latin, one in Swedish and then in Old and Modern Icelandic, one in Old English and then in fifteenth-century Scots and finally in Gothic. Finally, we also have a poem written in Gothic, 'Bagmē blōma', which will be given special attention here.

Songs for the Philologists was published by Tolkien and his friend and comrade Eric Valentine Gordon. They taught together at Leeds University from 1922 to 1925 and from 1924 worked together on the edition of *Sir Gawain and the Green Knight*, published the following year, which is still an authority in medieval English studies (1925). Together they founded a Viking Club, where they sang drinking and comedy songs with students.

1 - Presentation of 'Bagmē blōma'

The poem I am interested in here is entitled 'Bagmē blōma' i.e., "Flower of the Trees". It is a poem written in Neo-Gothic, i.e., in a language with non-Gothic words. The poem appears on page twelve of *Songs for the Philologists* and was reprinted in Tom Shippey's *Road to Middle-earth* (1992, 400). It should be noted in passing that the variants between the two editions are minor. Some misprints have crept into the collection published in 1936, especially in the Old English and Icelandic texts.

'Bagmē blōma' is structured in three sizains. The poem gives an insight into the extensive knowledge of Gothic that Tolkien had acquired since he had read, studied, and learned the language through the *Primer of the Gothic Language* by Joseph Wright, his professor of comparative linguistics at Oxford University (1910). His encounter with the language was an emotional shock for him and led him to create his own Gothic. Certainly, among all the languages he had learned and subsequently taught, Gothic was one that attracted him enormously. A good example of this can be seen in the many Gothic elements scattered throughout his legendarium. See for example the study by Arden R. Smith in the tribute volume to Richard E. Blackwelder (2006).

Gothic is an ancient Germanic language. It belongs to the family of Germanic languages, to the dialectal area called Ostic, as were the languages spoken by the Vandals, the Rugians, the Heruli, the Bastarnes, the Gepids, and the Burgundians, of whom no trace remains. From Gothic, on the other hand, we have a fragmented text, the Bible, which a bishop called Wulfila (311–382) translated from Greek or Latin into Gothic, with the aim of converting these Gothic speakers. The Gothic corpus consists mainly of the Bible, which Wulfila translated from Greek and Latin versions (Miller 2019). However, some 'minor' texts and a calendar have also come down to us. Among these documents, we find two deeds of sale; we also find the *Skeireins*, which is a commentary on the Gospel of John; finally, a palimpsest of the Old Testament was discovered in 2010 in the cathedral of Bologna, dating from the first half of the sixth century, i.e., written during the reign of Theodoric the Great in Ravenna (Rousseau 2015; Auer and de Vaan 2016; Falluomini 2014, 2017).

The interest of my study does not lie in linguistic analysis (Thöny 2005), nor in syntactic analysis (Annear 2011) of the Gothic poem. My approach is different: it seeks to demonstrate that Tolkien based his poem on passages from the Wulfila Bible, and more particularly on what we might call Gothic poetic elements.

2 - Gothic poetry

Tolkien dreamt of a 'lost' Gothic poetry. In *A Secret Vice*, he says: "There is purely artistic pleasure, keen and of a high order, in studying a Gothic dictionary from this point of view; and from it a part, one element of the pleasure which might have been gained from the resplendent 'lost Gothic' poetry may still be recaptured" (*Monsters*, 207). Tolkien understood, as does the philologist or historian of religion who is so often confronted with this, that ancient things are sometimes lost forever. We shall now see how Tolkien gives substance and life to this lost Gothic poetry.

At first sight, what is striking when reading 'Bagmē blōma' is the use of alliterative verse, common to all known ancient Germanic poetry. We can take the well-known Old English example of *Beowulf* to see that: "Hwæt! Wé Gardena in geárdagum,/ þéodcyninga, þrym gefrúnon,/ hu ða æþelingas ellen fremedon."

Alliteration can be either consonantal (the most frequent case), or vowelic, any vowel can alliterate with any other, sort of inner rhyme (*homoioteleuton*), etc.. To show that the Gothic poem follows this Germanic poetic tradition, alliterations of the first verse are underlined, and inner rhymes are in bold: "Brunaim bairiþ Bairka bogum."

As we can see throughout, Tolkien wrote a poem rich in alliteration, internal rhyme, and *homoioteleuton*. The stylistic development of the poem may have been due to contact with alliterative poems in Old English, Old Norse, or Old High German. However, it is possible to think that Tolkien drew his alliterative inspiration from the Gothic language itself.

3 - Alliteration in Gothic texts

The Gothic language is mainly known through the translation of the New Testament, probably from Greek and Latin models. When translating the Bible, Wulfila became immersed in the text and in its liturgy. It should be remembered that the biblical text had its own rhythmic pattern, so that it could be sung, if not chanted, by the clergy. Like other translators of the Bible, Wulfila was concerned with the rhythm of the liturgy and tried to preserve the musical language of Christian worship through translation.

In a long study on the style of the Gothic Bible published one century ago, the German philologist Friedrich Kauffmann demonstrated that it is in the liturgical parts of the Bible that the stylistic characteristics of the language are purest and clearest (Kauffmann 1920–1923). The translator of the Gothic Bible has endeavoured to reproduce the style of the psalms. This is achieved through three points: 1) the initial and final position of the verbs; 2) the repetition of the same idea (*parallelismus membrorum*); 3) the repetition of the same word (Kauffmann 1920, 14). Wulfila came very close to the Hellenistic style. But one may ask what influence he gave to the old Germanic traditions in his style. The answer lies primarily in the choice of words used by the translator, which sometimes belong to semantic spheres straight out of the ancient, pagan Germanic world. Thus, for the cosmic dimension, we find in some places the term *midjungard*, which will become *Miðgarðr* in Old Icelandic or, in English, and particularly in Tolkien, *Middle-earth*. There is also vocabulary borrowed from the anthropocentric domain, the socio–legal domain, as well as the magical–sacred domain (Rousseau 2012, 282-95). Apart from this recourse to ancient semantic spheres, one cannot ignore Wulfila's use of ornamental forms of representation and the rhythmic values of his writing. Wulfila's Bible has a colorimetry that is related to the rhythmic cadences of the old Germanic alliterative verse. Wulfila did not compose long alliterative verses, as in *Beowulf* or the so-called *Poetic Edda*, but he made the pre–literary verbal art and poetic rhythm of Gothic oral literature legible and audible.

Since the beginning of the 19th century, philologists have found dozens of examples of alliterative passages. The first were Hans Stolzenburg (Stolzenburg 1905) and Friedrich Kauffmann in 1920's, who published in the *Zeitschrift für deutsche Philologie*. Afterwards, some of them took up the issue again, without bringing any new data (Ambrosini 1967; Toporova 1989; Wolfe 2006; Rousseau 2012, 152-3; Miller 2019, 14-5, 109-10). With these philologists, a certain importance was given to the alliteration found in great numbers in the Gothic text. This led them to speak of a 'poetic enthusiastic breath'. It is clear that Wulfila had made himself responsible for something that is partly due to his language. The alliteration did not need to be artfully inserted by the translator; such occurrences presented themselves to him without his having sought them out. It seemed natural to Wulfila to use alliteration. To what degree was he aware of this? It is hard to say. However, alliteration exists, consciously or unconsciously inserted into the Gothic translation.

Tolkien may have seen how alliterative the Bible could be in many places. When we look at 'Bagmē blōma', we can assume that Tolkien, to give his poem a poetic breath, drew inspiration from certain passages in the Bible. Looking closely at the Gothic text, I have found a few passages (Streitberg 1908) which could coincide with Tolkien's: sometimes in spirit, sometimes in the use of alliterative terms:

Biblical references	Gothic verses	'Bagmē blōma's' verses
Mt. 7:25	waiwoun windos	v.7: wopjand windos
G. 6:5	baurþein bairiþ	v.1: brunain bairiþ bairka bogum
Ti. 6:15	þiudans þiudanondane	v.12: þiuda meina þiuþjandei
Ti. 6:15	frauja fraujinondane	v.6/18: fraujinondei fairguni
Mk. 16:17	razdom rodjand	v.10: razda rodeiþ
1Cor. 14:23	rodjand razdom	v.10: razda rodeiþ

There are, in all likelihood, parallels that can be drawn.

4 - *Figura etymologica* in Gothic

Tolkien may have been inspired by alliterative passages in the Bible to compose 'Bagmē blōma'. Finally, I would like to add that he went even further, using what Gothic philologists call the *figura etymologica*. The etymological figure is a very old construction, often in the form of a formulary, and attested in Indo-European poetry. The German linguist Rüdiger Schmitt devoted his doctoral thesis to this reconstructed poetry and the Indo-European formulary (Schmitt 1967, 264-6). The etymological figure is a syntactic construction consisting of elements all belonging to the same root, as we find several examples in the Gothic Bible. Thus, *wulfos wilwandans* (Matthew, 7:15) "wolves devouring (their prey)" i.e., "predatory wolves". *Wulfs* "wolf" and *wilwan* "to ravish, to plunder" have an obvious assonance, which perhaps goes back to a common etymology (**wḷkw* for *wulfs*, **welkw* for *wilwan*).

It should be noted that the linguist Ferdinand de Saussure, in an article entitled "Gotique *wilwan*", writes the following: "It was most probably from the verb **welk2ō* that the primitive language had derived **wḷk2o-s* 'the wolf', which for the Arian [Wulfila] was always synonymous with brigand. The vague feeling of this kinship perhaps still remained when Ulfilas [Wulfila] wrote *wulfs frawilwiþ, wulfos wilwandans* (John, 10:12; Matthew, 7:15)" (Saussure 1889).

In verse 14 of 'Bagmē blōma', Tolkien creates from scratch an etymological figure: *liuhteiþ liuhmam lauhmuni* (literally: "shines in grapes of light the lightning"). These three words have the same Indo-European root **lewk–*, which means "to shine" (Holthausen 1934, 61, 64). The word *liuhmam* is Tolkien's creation, based on the word **liuhma*, probably to be

compared with the Old English *lēoma* "ray of light, beam",
the Old Norse *ljómi* "light" or the Latin *lumen* "light" (Thöny
2005, 3). At this stage of the study, I do not know whether
Tolkien was aware that he was producing such a work which
mixed poetry and philology to the highest degree, especially
when we know, since Verlyn Flieger's study *Splintered Light*,
how fundamental the notion of 'light' was in Tolkien's work.
If Tolkien was fully aware of what he was doing, then he had
created a work which went beyond the simple poem sung in a
pub with students to make historical philology more attractive
and accessible to them.

5 - Conclusion

For Tolkien, poetry is synonymous with language, and the one
cannot be separated from the other. At the end of this paper, I
think we can better understand Tolkien's words when he writes
the following in *A Secret Vice*: "There is purely artistic pleasure,
keen and of a high order, in studying a Gothic dictionary from
this point of view; and from it a part, one element, of the
pleasure which might have been gained from the resplendent
'lost Gothic' poetry may still be recaptured" (*Monsters*, 207).

Bibliography

Ambrosini, Riccardo, 'Di alcune caratteristiche semantiche e prosodiche nelle traduzioni dei Vangeli in gotico ed in slavo antico', *Studi e saggi linguistici*, 7 (1967), 76-105.

Annear, Lucas, 'Language in Tolkien's *Bagmē blōma*', *Tolkien Studies* 8 (2011), 37-49.

Le Palimpseste gotique de Bologne. Études philologiques et linguistiques, ed. Anita Auer and Michiel de Vaan (Lausanne: Cahier de l'I.L.S.L., 2016).

Falluomini, Carla, 'Zum gotischen Fragment aus Bologna', *Zeitschrift für deutsches Altertum und deutsche Literatur*, 143 (2014), 281-305.
—, 'Zum gotischen Fragment aus Bologna II: Berichtigungen und neue Lesungen', *Zeitschrift für deutsches Altertum und deutsche Literatur*, 146 (2017), 284-294.

Holthausen, Ferdinand, *Gotisches Etymologisches Wörterbuch*, (Heidelberg: Carl Winters Universitätsbuchhandlung, 1934).

Kauffmann, Friedrich, 'Der stil der gotischen Bibel (I-III)', *Zeitschrift für deutsche Philologie*, 48 (1920), 7-80, 165-235, 349-388.
—, 'Der stil der gotischen Bibel (IV)', *Zeitschrift für deutsche Philologie*, 49 (1923), 11-57.

Miller, D. Gary, *The Oxford Gothic Grammar*, (Oxford: Oxford University Press, 2019).

Rousseau, André, *Grammaire explicative du gotique*, (Paris: L'Harmattan, 2012).
—, 'Un nouveau manuscrit gotique découvert à Bologne (*Codex Bononiensis*)', *Études Germaniques*, 279 (2015), 431-449.

Saussure, Ferdinand de, 'Gotique *wilwan*', *Mémoires de la Société de Linguistique,* 6 (1889), 358.

Shippey, Tom, *The Road to Middle-earth* (London: HarperCollins, 1992).

Smith, Arden R., 'Tolkienian Gothic', in *The Lord of the Rings 1954-2004: Scholarship in Honor of Richard E. Blackwelder*, ed. by Wayne G. Hammond and Christina Scull (Milwaukee: Marquette University Press, 2006), pp. 267-281.

Schmitt, Rüdiger, *Dichtung und Dichtersprache in indogermanischer Zeit,* (Wiesbaden: Otto Harrassowitz, 1967).

Stolzenburg, Hans, 'Zur Übersetzungstechnik des Wulfila untersucht auf Grund der Bibelfragmente des *Codex Argenteus*', *Zeitschrift für deutsche Philologie,* 37 (1905), 145-93, 352-392.

Streitberg, Wilhelm, *Die gotische Bibel,* (Heidelberg: Carl Winters Universitätsbuchhandlung, 1908).

Thöny, Luzius, '*Bagmē blōma* by J.R.R. Tolkien: Grammatische Analyse', 2005, 1-3 <https://www.swanrad.ch/downloads/bagmēblōma_kom.pdf>

Tolkien, J.R.R., Gordon, E.V., *Sir Gawain and the Green Knight,* (Oxford: Oxford University Press, 1925).
—, *Songs for the Philologists,* (London: Department of English at University College, 1936).

Tolkien, J.R.R., *The Monsters and the Critics and Other Essays*, ed. by Christopher Tolkien (London: George Allen & Unwin, 1983).

Toporova, Tat'jana Vladimirovna, 'Problema original'nosti: Gotskie složnye slova i fragment teksta', *Voprosy jazykoznanija,* 38 (1989), 64-76.

Wolfe, Brendan N., '*Figurae etymologicae* in Gothic', *Oxford University Working Papers in Linguistics, Philology & Phonetics* 11 (2006), 207-214.

Wright, Joseph, *A Primer of the Gothic Language: With Grammar, Notes and Glossary,* (Oxford: Oxford University Press, 1910).

Beware Melkors Bearing Gifts: The 'Tale of Adanel' as Gothic Fiction

Kristine Larsen

1 - Introduction

One of the philosophically densest of Tolkien's post-*Lord of the Rings* writings[1] is 'Athrabeth Finrod ah Andreth', published in *The History of Middle-earth Volume X: Morgoth's Ring*, a conversation about mortality, fate, and Elf/Human relationships. Andreth, a human woman, hints at an incident from the distant past of her kind, "before any had yet died" (*Morgoth*, 345), in which they greatly disappointed Eru, the deity, resulting, they believe, in their mortality (or at the very least a great reduction of their lifespan). This event, which they "have tried to forget" is detailed in Tolkien's Author's notes to the 'Tale of Adanel' (313).[2] While the 'Tale of Adanel' was never published in Tolkien's lifetime, and, like the 'Athrabeth' itself was not included in the official 1977 published *Silmarillion* edited by Christopher Tolkien, there are subtle references to its central events in that work, events Tolkien makes brief references to in several of his letters (141, 259). For example, in a famous 1951 letter to Milton Waldman he notes of humans in Middle-earth that there is "a rumour that for a while they fell under

---

1. Christopher Tolkien dates the writing of 'Athrabeth' to the mid to late 1950s (*Morgoth*, 304).

2. The main text, notes, and revisions of the 'Tale of Adanel' can be found in *Morgoth's Ring*, 351-60.

the domination of the Enemy and that some repented" (*Letters*, Letter 131, 147-8). These repeated references suggest that Tolkien considered the fall of humans in his legendarium settled canon, as much as anything could be in the legendarium, writing in an author's note to 'Athrabeth' that the 'Tale of Adanel' is "no doubt mainly derived from actual lore of the People of Marach" (*Morgoth*, 344).

I must begin my analysis with a disclaimer. I intend to avoid commenting on the thorny philosophical and theological issues that are central to the 'Athrabeth' and, by connection, the 'Tale of Adanel', as much as is possible. Instead, I will simply argue that the 'Tale of Adanel' is one of Tolkien's most Gothic tales.

2 - A Summary of the 'Tale of Adanel'

As many readers may not be familiar with the 'Tale of Adanel', I include an overview for convenience. The narrator recounts how a Voice – Eru – had spoken to early humans, urging them to "be children and learn" (*Morgoth*, 345). However, humans were predictably un-Entish and hasty, and "desired to order things to our will" (346), quickly becoming dissatisfied with Eru's pedagogical style, which stressed individual responsibility, critical thinking, and active learning in order to "first seek to find the answer for yourself" (345). In other words, they desired, like too many students today, to be spoon-fed the answers, because "learning was difficult" (345). Do we perhaps spy an echo of Tolkien the frustrated professor here? Regardless, their impatience left humans easy pickings for Melkor, who appeared "in our own form, but greater and more beautiful" and promised them instant intellectual and technological gratification – including better food and dwellings – through the "marvellous riches which knowledge can unlock" if they would just trust this self-described "Giver of Gifts" (346). As in the case of breaking the prohibition against eating from the Tree of Knowledge of Good and Evil in the Old Testament, ignoring Eru's instruction to "not seek to leave childhood before your time" leads to naught but grief. Not surprisingly, their new fair friend was "less swift than we had hoped" to pass along information, and because he had "awakened many desires in our hearts" easily "enthralled" them, as they feared a return to their original "poor and hard" life (346). Boasting that he had come "out of the Dark, but I am Its master" (and additionally claiming to have created the sun, moon, and stars), Melkor offered to protect humans from the Darkness and the original Voice, which he claimed was that of the Darkness itself (346).

In a scene reminiscent of Mark Twain's *A Connecticut Yankee in King Arthur's Court* (1889), and the original edition[3] of H. Rider Haggard's *King Solomon's Mines* (1885), a total solar eclipse – "when the Sun's light began to fail, until it was blotted out and a great shadow fell on the world" (347) – caused fear among the astronomically ignorant humans, allowing Melkor to bolster his claim of celestial powers. Noting that some among them still listened to the Voice, he demanded the building of a great temple where he could be worshiped. Afterwards, having wrapped the humans around his no-longer fair appearing fingers, he demanded more from his thralls, including the committing of "worse" deeds (347).

Meanwhile the Voice of Eru visited the humans one night, reprimanding his wayward children: "I gave you life. Now it shall be shortened, and each of you in a little while come to Me,

---

3. The event was changed to a lunar eclipse in subsequent editions due to Haggard's realization that he had made a number of significant astronomical errors in describing the solar eclipse.

to learn who is your Lord: the one ye worship, or I who made him" (347). In response, humans began to fear the Darkness even more, especially when some of them began to "die in horror and anguish" (347). For his part, their chosen Lord lacked concern for his dead minions because "otherwise there would soon be too many of you, crawling like lice on the Earth" (348). Instead, he threatened to kill any who disobeyed him.

Tired, hungry, and sick, shunned by other living creatures and threatened by the natural forces of fire and water, humanity realized too late that it had backed the wrong horse. In their hatred and fear they continued to do Melkor's bidding, hoping in vain to avoid further torture or even death at his hands. The cruelest among them were rewarded, while those who openly spoke out against their Master were hunted by their brethren and committed to the fire if caught. Those few who escaped into other lands could not escape the wrath of Eru, nor ultimately the cruelty of Melkor. Here the 'Tale of Adanel' rejoins the standard history of the First Age in *The Silmarillion*, for example when Bëor the Old explains to Finrod that his people know little of their history, save that "A darkness lies behind us [...] and we have turned our backs upon it, and we do not desire to return thither even in thought" (*Silmarillion*, 141), a history similarly echoed in the start of 'Akallabêth' (259).[4]

3 - Gothic Themes in the 'Tale of Adanel'

Which characteristics code this tale as distinctively Gothic? Similarities between this 'Tale of Adanel' and 'Akallabêth', in particular human worship of Melkor as Lord of the Darkness (in 'Akallabêth' due to the influence of Sauron), are interesting,

---

4. It is also alluded to in the original text of 'The Drowning of Anadûnê' (*Sauron*, 341).

although certainly not unexpected, as Tolkien was working on the two works at roughly the same time (*Morgoth*, 304; *Peoples*, 141-2) and had written the direct precursor to 'Akallabêth', 'The Drowning of Anadûnê', a decade before (*Sauron*, 147). Tolkien openly admits in one of his author's notes to 'Athrabeth' that the 'Tale of Adanel' "bears certain resemblances to the Númenórean traditions concerning the part played by Sauron in the downfall of Númenor", something that is to be expected because the "operations of Sauron naturally and inevitably resembled or repeated those of his master" (*Morgoth*, 344). As part of his 'Silmarillion Primer', Jeff LaSala tackles the fall of Númenor as described in 'Akallabêth', drawing comparisons with Mary Shelley's famous Gothic novel, *Frankenstein* (1818), terming Númenóreans' attempts to "discover if they might the secret of recalling life, or at the least of the prolonging of Men's days" (*Silmarillion*, 266) a "delightful little Frankenstein part of the story" (2018). There are also overlaps with the second part of the incomplete time travel tale 'The Notion Club Papers', in which the members of the club begin to make connections with past lives. As Verlyn Flieger notes in *A Question of Time*, it is "here that the story takes on its gothic tinge. It becomes in this respect strongly reminiscent of the spiritual thrillers of Tolkien's fellow Inkling Charles Williams" (151). These writings are also contemporaneous, and closely aligned with, the writing of 'The Drowning of Anadûnê' (*Sauron*, 147).

Anna Kędra-Kardela and Andrzej Kowalczyk note that Gothic novels are "often presented to the reader as an 'ancient' [...] document of unknown authorship or a fragment of a manuscript discovered in some shadowy circumstances" (2014, 20-1). The 'Tale of Adanel' certainly fits this trope, describing events about which Andreth warns Finrod "the Wise are uncertain and speak with contrary voices" (*Morgoth*,

313). The atmosphere of mystery surrounding the events in the 'Tale of Adanel' fits well with that in others of Tolkien's contemporaneous writings (e.g. *Morgoth*, 343, 373) in describing the mythology of the *Silmarillion* tradition as a "Mannish' affair" reflecting human biases (370). In one of his own author's notes to 'Athrabeth', Tolkien explains that while Andreth reveals very little about this unfortunate history to Finrod, "longer recensions of the *Athrabeth*, evidently edited under Númenórean influence, make her give, under pressure, a more precise answer", perhaps referring to the text of the 'Tale of Adanel' itself (344). Tolkien further explains that all of these supposed revised histories concur that the cause of the fall of humanity is "the acceptance of Men by Melkor as King (or King and God)" (344). Interestingly, while, as previously noted, Tolkien felt the 'Tale of Adanel' to be "no doubt mainly derived" from legends of the Edain,[5] in an added note he admits that "Nothing is hereby asserted concerning its 'truth', historical or otherwise" (344).[6] To explain this comment further would necessitate an analysis of the theology of the legendarium and mortality as the "gift of Ilúvatar" (*Silmarillion*, 42), which conveniently places it beyond the purview of this analysis.

Gothic plots typically feature a villain who threatens "a distressed, isolated damsel (a virgin), usually of aristocratic origin, beautiful and pure" as well as murder and mayhem (Kędra-Kardela and Kowalczyk 2014, 22). Villain – check. Murder and mayhem – check. In a symbolic sense the newly awakened humans resemble naïve damsels, and Melkor is

---

5. In the c.1968 essay 'Notes on Órë' Tolkien offers that the 'Athrabeth' (including the 'Tale of Adanel') "appears to have been actually of Mannish origin probably deriving from Andreth herself (*Nature*, 222).

6. Tolkien conveniently sets up this ambivalence by starting the 'Tale of Adanel' with the famous signal phrase "Some say" (*Morgoth*, 345).

certainly guilty of robbing them of their spiritual virginity. Supernatural phenomenon and atmospheres of "gloom, horror and mystery" are also heightened by the appearance of threatening natural phenomenon (21),[7] paralleling common childhood fears of "darkness, storms, thunder, and strange events" (Taylor and Arnow 1988, 23). Not coincidentally, these are the precise fears demonstrated by these so-named Second Children of Ilúvatar and easily manipulated by Melkor. In particular, darkness, nocturnal settings, and shadows play an important role in Gothic literature, and in a metaphorical sense "threatened the light of reason with what it did not know" (Botting 2013, 30).[8]

Due to the rarity of fear-inspiring events in which the life-giving sun is suddenly swallowed during the day, solar eclipses are the perfect storm of darkness and shadow, as reflected in the historical and literary records. For example, a solar eclipse viewed from the Middle-east on June 15, 763 BCE has been suggested as the genesis of an episode in *Amos* 8:9 in which God warned sinners that He would "make the sun go down at noon and darken the earth in broad daylight" (Espenak). The *Anglo-Saxon Chronicles* also linked historical eclipses to terrible events. For example, in the year 664 it was said that "there was an eclipse of the sun on 3 May; and in this year

---

7. See Larsen, 'Shadow and Flame', for a detailed examination of examples in the legendarium.
8. Kędra-Kardela and Kowalczyk (2014, 22) also note that a number of famous Gothic authors were reportedly motivated to write by a personal haunting dream (including Mary Shelley and Bram Stoker). As is well-known, Tolkien's legend of the downfall of Númenor was inspired by his "complex" or "Atlantis haunting", as he called it (*Letters*, Letter 180, 232; Letter 257, 347). He exorcized this personal demon by writing about it, including transferring the dream to Faramir in *The Return of the King* (*Letters*, Letter 163, 213).

a great pestilence came to the island of Britain, and in that pestilence Bishop Tuda died", as well as "Eorcenberht, king of the people of Kent" (Whitelock 1961, 21). In *The Silmarillion*, the metaphor of an eclipse is also used to evoke a sense of impending doom. On the day of Beren's death, it is said that "a dark shadow" fell upon Lúthien, and "it seemed to her that the sun had sickened and turned black" (*Silmarillion*, 185). In the mythology of Middle-earth[9] solar eclipses are caused by the unrequited infatuation of Tilion, the driver of the moon, for the radiant Arien, who piloted the sun, resulting in his deviating from the path and speed commanded by Varda. Because of this, "at times it will chance that he comes so nigh that his shadow cuts off her brightness and there is a darkness amid the day" (101). However, it would not be uncharacteristic of Melkor to take advantage of this natural event to scare the inexperienced humans, "walking through the shadow like a bright fire" (*Morgoth*, 347). Such a vision aligns with Anne Petty's observation of evil in Tolkien's world as frequently depicted as "shadow and flame" (2003, 99), the balrog of Khazad-dûm being a classic example (*FR*, 'The Mirror of Galadriel', 371).

Given the depth of the fear and horror associated with the Gothic environment, it is not surprising that strong feelings are likewise described in the language of the literature, for example through the use of terms such as "affliction, agony, alarm, amazement, anguish, choler, dismay, dread, fright, fury [...] thunderstruck, wrathful, and the like" (Kędra-Kardela and Kowalczyk 2014, 23). A simple term frequency analysis of the words included in the 'Tale of Adanel' demonstrates the relative numerical importance of certain specific words, including "voice" (15 instances, 14 in a supernatural sense)

---

9. See Larsen, 'Darkness Amid the Day', for a detailed analysis of Tolkien's use of solar and lunar eclipses in the legendarium.

"dark" (13 instances) and "gift/s" (8 instances). However, by grouping terms with similar meanings, clearer Gothic patterns emerge, as seen in Table 1. Note that both strong emotions and atmospheric terms have a strong showing. Interestingly, while terms associated with *learn* appear 14 times, *teach* only appears 7 times. It appears the humans learned on their own in the end after all.[10]

Table 1: Frequency of word meaning clusters

Word Meaning	Frequency
Dark (e.g. dark, darkness, shadow, night)	23
Master (e.g. master, command, Lord)	21
Affliction (e.g. trouble, hunger, sickness)	21
Serve (e.g. appease, revered, bow, worship)	19
Gifts (e.g. gift, giving, bring)	16
Power (e.g. powerful, strong, great)	14
Voice (in supernatural sense)	14
Fear (e.g. fearing, afraid, dread, terror)	14
Learn (e.g. learn, knowledge, understand)	14
Death (e.g. die, slay, devour)	12
Desire (e.g. yearned, wished, desired)	10
Fire (e.g. fire, flame, scorched)	8
Injury (e.g. assailed, shortened)	8

10. Readers interested in word frequency and emotion prevalence analysis of *The Silmarillion, The Hobbit*, and *The Lord of the Rings* are directed to the LOTR Project's keyword frequency (http://lotrproject.com/statistics/books/keywordsearch) and sentiment analysis (http://lotrproject.com/statistics/books/sentimentanalysis) pages.

Anger (e.g. angry, hatred)	7
Teach (e.g. taught, teacher, show)	7
Pain (e.g. anguish, despair, weariness)	7

The frequency of terms related to "desire" is of particular interest, as in Gothic works we often find a "relation between prohibition and desire, [as] transgression involves a crossing of limits or breaking of taboos and rules" including "disobeying paternal injunctions" (Botting 2013, 9). Tolkien is clear about the reason for the fall of humans – they desired to acquire knowledge too quickly, openly disobeying the limits set upon them by their father, Ilúvatar. According to the legend, the punishment meted out for this disobedience was either the beginning of their mortality, or a great shortening of their lifespans. Similarly, Dimitra Fimi points out that the lifespan of the Númenóreans began to diminish – "their years lessened" (*RK*, 'Appendix A', 316) – when they "began to long for immortality as a sign of the withdrawal of the favour of the Valar" (Fimi 2010, 148).

4 - Degeneration in the 'Tale of Adanel'

Note that as in the case of classic Gothic literature, the 'Tale of Adanel' is set in the past, as compared with the present of the 'Athrabeth', in this case so ancient that, as Andreth admits, "we cannot remember any time when we were not as we are – save only legends of days when death came less swiftly and our span was still far longer, but already there was death" (*Morgoth*, 313). Katarzyna Ferdynus reflects that Gothic tales are set in the past in order to exploit a setting of a "deteriorated world" that is "the source of terror and haunting" (2016, 35-6).

This deterioration is not only physical, but moral and spiritual as well, a *fallen* world in all senses of the word. Such a concept is also central to the mythology of Middle-earth, the world known as Arda Marred thanks to the machinations of Melkor interwoven into the very song of creation. As Tolkien offered in the 1951 letter to Milton Waldman, "there cannot be any 'story' without a fall – all stories are ultimately about the fall" (*Letters*, Letter 131, 147).[11]

In theological discussions, the "retrogressive changes" in humans due to their fall from their original Edenic state of perfection are sometimes termed *degeneration* (Walter 1956, 422). A more pseudo-scientific treatment gained traction in some quarters in the middle of the 19th century, in particular as championed by the work of Bénédict Augustin Morel in his *Treatise on the Degeneration of the Human Species* (1857). Utilizing a Lamarckian model of evolution, Morel argued that mental degradation of individuals caused by an environment steeped in poverty, alcoholism, and pollution would be passed down to their children, causing increased degeneracy and "congenital idiocy and sterility" by the fourth generation (Hurley 1996, 66). Not surprisingly, Morel's ideas resonated with the eugenics movement (Walter 1956, 427). Degeneration was seen as a type of reverse evolution, as evolution was often (and quite erroneously) depicted as the linear, directed, upward march of life – especially humans – from more primitive (and hence less "fit") toward more complex (and, it was reasoned, more "fit") forms. As Kelly Hurley argues "Degenerationism […] is a 'gothic' discourse, and as such is a crucial imaginative

---

11. The ultimate fate of Arda Marred, including its ultimate healing or re-creation, was a topic very much on Tolkien's mind during the 1950s, and is one of the important philosophical/theological topics of discussion in 'Athrabeth'.

and narrative source for the *fin-de-siècle* Gothic" (1996, 65). As such, the "ruination" of humans is "practiced insistently, almost obsessively, in the pages of British Gothic fiction" (3).[12]

Hurley offers the example of the Eloi and Morlocks in H.G. Wells' 1895 novella *The Time Machine*, these degenerated humans – mentioned directly by Tolkien in a 1947 letter to Stanley Unwin (*Letters*, Letter 109, 121) – existing in an imagined far distant future (81). Tolkien himself utilizes the concept of evolutionary degeneration in his myriad discussions of the origin of the Orcs. (e.g. *Letters*, Letter 210, 274; *Morgoth*, 47, 78, 409, 413; *RK*, 'The Tower of Cirith Ungol', 190). Having decided that, as the origin of Dwarves at the hand of the Vala Aulë demonstrated, "only Eru could make creatures with independent wills, and with reasoning powers" (*Morgoth*, 409), since evil cannot create it must corrupt, and therefore degenerate pre-existing species.[13] The spiritual degeneration of humans in the 'Tale of Adanel', leading (it is claimed) to the physical degeneration of humans in terms of their lifespan (and perhaps even their very mortality), thus also brands this as a Gothic tale.

---

12. Hurley borrows the term "abhuman" from supernaturalist author William Hope Hodgson to describe these degenerated humans, and connects the concept with Julia Kristeva's formulation of "abjection" (1996, 3-4).

13. Dimitra Fimi explores the racial "degeneration" of Orcs in *Tolkien, Race and Cultural History* (2010, 154-7). She points out that Tolkien's description of Orcs as "degraded and repulsive versions of the (to Europeans) least lovely Mongol-types" (*Letters*, Letter 210, 274) appears to "reflect popular ideas of the traditional hierarchy of the three extreme human racial types: the Caucasoid, the Mongoloid and the Negroid" (Fimi 2010, 156). This hierarchy developed from the concept of "monogemism" in the scientific racism paradigm of the 19th century, which assumed that the three main races represent varying levels of degeneration from the original perfection of Adam and Eve. It is, of course, assumed that Caucasians represent the smallest level of degeneration, and hence the closest relationship with divine perfection (Gould 1981, 39-40). See Keel (2013) for an overview of these ideas in our Primary World.

5 - Conclusion: The Ultimate Lesson of the 'Tale of Adanel'

In a 1947 letter to Stanley Unwin, Tolkien explained that "every romance that takes things seriously must have a warp of fear and horror, if however remotely or representatively it is to resemble reality, and not be mere escapism" (Letters, Letter 109, 120). Accordingly, he found "great comfort" in the fact that he had "managed to make the horror really horrible" in his subcreation, a rather Gothic viewpoint (120). In particular, the 'Tale of Adanel' certainly demonstrates this "warp of fear and horror" (120). At the same time, in reflecting on the fall of humanity in this Secondary World we are allowed a brief nostalgic glimpse of Eden, which Tolkien mused in a 1945 letter to his son Christopher "We all long for [...] our whole nature at its best and least corrupted, its gentlest and most humane" (*Letters*, Letter 96, 110). However, as he notes, while we yearn for a return to our original nature, "We shall never recover it, for that is not the way of repentance", although we may "recover something like it" (110). We see this reflected in Tolkien's imagined world in "the peoples of the West" in whom

> the good side are Re-formed. That is they are the descendants of Men that tried to repent and fled Westward from the domination of the Prime Dark Lord, and his false worship, and by contrast with the Elves renewed (and enlarged) their knowledge of the truth and the nature of the World. (*Letters*, Letter 156, 204)

Indeed, in *The Silmarillion* we read how after encountering the Elves in Beleriand, the humans who became known as the Elf-friends "learned swiftly of the Eldar all such art and knowledge as they could receive, and their sons increased in wisdom and skill, until they far surpassed all others of Mankind, who dwelt still east of the mountains" (*Silmarillion*, 149).

Furthermore, 'Akallabêth' summarizes that at the end of the First Age as a reward for fighting against the forces of Morgoth, their old enemy, the Edain are not only gifted the island of Númenor but are personally taught by Eönwë, the herald of Manwë, and to them are given "wisdom and power and life more enduring than any others of mortal race have possessed" (260). But as Tolkien wisely mused to Milton Waldman, "Reward on earth is more dangerous for men than punishment!" (*Letters*, Letter 131, 154). How ironic for humans to finally receive the knowledge they had so craved only for much of it to be squandered and perverted once more in the fall of Númenor, in yet another Gothic   of decline and darkness. As Tolkien reflected of the cautionary nature of the 'Tale of Adanel', "That a people in possession of such a legend or tradition should have later been deluded by Sauron is sad but, in view of human history generally, not incredible" (*Morgoth*, 344).

Bibliography

Botting, Fred, *Gothic*, 2nd ed., (London and New York: Routledge, 2013).

Espenak, Fred, *Solar Eclipses of Historical Interest*, NASA Eclipse Website, 28 September 2009, < https://eclipse.gsfc.nasa.gov/SEhistory/SEhistory.html> [accessed 7 December 2022].

Ferdynus, Katarzyna, 'The Shadow of the Past. *The Lord of the Rings* and the Gothic Novel', *New Horizons in English Studies*, 1 (2016), 32-42.

Fimi, Dimitra, *Tolkien, Race and Cultural History*, (New York: Palgrave Macmillan, 2010).

Flieger, Verlyn, *A Question of Time*, (Kent: The Kent State University Press, 1997).

Gould. Stephen Jay, *The Mismeasure of Man*, (New York: W.W. Norton and Co., 1981).

Hurley, Kelly, *The Gothic Body: Sexuality, Materialism, and Degeneration at the Fin De Siècle*, (Cambridge: Cambridge University Press, 1996).

Kędra-Kardela, Anna, and Andrzej Slawomir Kowalczyk, 'The Gothic Canon', in *Expanding the Gothic Canon*, ed. by Anna Kędra-Kardela and Andrzej Slawomir Kowalczyk (Frankfurt: Peter Lang, 2014), pp. 13-39.

Keel, Terence D., 'Religion, Polygenism and the Early Science of Human Origins', *History of the Human Sciences*, 26.2 (2013), 3-22.

Larsen, Kristine, 'Shadow and Flame: Myth, Monsters, and Mother Nature in Middle-earth', in *The Mirror Crack'd: Fear and Horror in J.R.R. Tolkien's* The Lord of the Rings *and its Sources*, ed. by Lynn Forest-Hill (Newcastle upon Tyne: Cambridge Scholars Publishing, 2008), pp. 169-196.
— '"Darkness Amid the Day": Eclipses in the Works of J.R.R. Tolkien', *Amon Hen*, 276 (2019), 8-12.

LaSala, Jeff, *A Farewell to Kings: The Fall of Númenor*, Tor, 31 October 2018, <https://www.tor.com/2018/10/31/a-farewell-to-kings-the-fall-of-numenor/> [accessed 7 December 2022].

Petty, Anne C., *Tolkien in the Land of Heroes*, (Cold Spring Harbor: Cold Spring Press, 2003).

Taylor, C. Barr, and Bruce Arnow, *The Nature and Treatment of Anxiety Disorders*, (New York: Macmillan, 1988).

Tolkien, J.R.R., *The Fellowship of the Ring*, (Boston: Houghton Mifflin, 1993).
— *Morgoth's Ring*, ed. by Christopher Tolkien (Boston: Houghton Mifflin, 1993).
— *The Return of the King*, (Boston: Houghton Mifflin, 1993).
— *The Peoples of Middle-earth*, ed. by Christopher Tolkien (Boston: Houghton Mifflin, 1996).
— *The Letters of J.R.R. Tolkien*, ed. by Humphrey Carpenter (Boston: Houghton Mifflin, 2000).
— *The Silmarillion*, ed. by Christopher Tolkien (Boston: Houghton Mifflin, 2001).
— *Sauron Defeated*, ed. by Christopher Tolkien (London: HarperCollins, 2002).
— *The Nature of Middle-earth*, ed. by Carl Hostetter (Boston: Houghton Mifflin Harcourt, 2021).

Walter, Richard D., 'What Became of the Degenerate? A Brief History of a Concept', *Journal of the History of Medicine and Allied Sciences*, 11.4 (1956): 422-429.

Whitelock, Dorothy, *The Anglo-Saxon Chronicle*, (London: Eyre and Spottis Woode, 1961).

Eldritch Tolkien: The Impossibility of the Gothic in Middle-earth[1]

Nick Groom (Keynote)

Today, most people in the English-speaking world associate the Gothic with eighteenth and nineteenth-century terror fiction and twentieth and twenty-first-century horror films; these are linked through style and taste to the Gothic subculture of fashion, music, and attitude – remarkably, these Goths have been around since the late 1970s and the subculture shows no sign of abating, with regular performances, clubs, and festivals held in the UK and Europe, as well as North America and Japan. Gothic is also the defining style of mediaeval architecture, revived in the nineteenth century and evident in much of the built environment across Britain and Ireland – from country churches to the Palace of Westminster. There were also earlier Goths – the ancient Germanic tribes that conquered the Romans. These different meanings of Gothic and the Goths are not entirely unrelated. My own work on the Gothic treats it as an historicist movement, combining cultural and political understandings of the term; moreover, I argue that the Gothic

1. My thanks are due to The Tolkien Society and Shaun Gunnar, to Lynn Forest-Hill and Martin Simonson, to Jennifer Brooker, Chris Walsh, and Jessica Yates, and especially to Will Sherwood. This paper was first given before the publication of the first edition of my book *Twenty-First-Century Tolkien: What Middle-Earth Means To Us Today* (London: Atlantic Books, 2022), and while covering some similar material this essay focuses on distinctively Gothic elements.

was, to a degree, a characteristically English style of literature, architecture, art, and folklore that emerged from politicized cultural memories (Groom 2012).

To begin, then, at the beginning. The Goths who sacked Rome and overran the Roman Empire in the fifth century AD were seen in two ways: as the destroyers of classical arts and learning, but also as champions of liberty rebelling against Roman tyranny, imperialism, and decadence, consequently representing a vibrant Northern alternative to the Mediterranean axis of civilization. They also established their own European empire from Italy to Spain, and developed a culture that would influence European thinking throughout the Middle Ages. The central figure here is the philosopher Boethius, whose ideas, as Tom Shippey and others have shown, pervade *The Lord of the Rings* (Shippey 2000, 133-8). These two versions of the Goths – either as barbarians or as freedom fighters – were elaborated over the next thousand years. In the Renaissance, which revived classical learning, anything non-classical was declared barbaric, so mediaeval architecture, from Norman churches to perpendicular chapels with all their characteristics of pointed arches, ribbed vaulting, flying buttresses, and organic ornamentation, was deemed to be barbarous and consequently 'Gothic'. Alongside this, however, the love of freedom that had led to the Goths rebelling against Rome seemed to be repeated at significant moments in history. English history was theorized as progressive, in which tyrannical and repressive authority was resisted through the 'Gothic spirit' – prime examples being the Magna Carta of 1215, which limited the sovereign's power by creating an English Parliament to balance and moderate the governance of the people, or the Reformation, which broke with Roman Catholicism and Papal authority to assert identity and independence through national institutions such as the established Anglican Church as well as the monarch, the Lords, and the Commons. So the idea of a 'Gothic constitution' of King and Parliament emerged, promoting individual rights and liberties and endorsing an ongoing extension of social values. This coalesced into a political ideology that supported parliament and Protestantism, and then personal independence, entrepreneurship, commerce, and imperialism, and finally emerged in the arts as a fashion for originality and creativity as an alternative to imitating classical models, and a revival of the styles and subjects of the non-classical Middle Ages. This political ideology was that of the 'Whig' Party, a party that dominated eighteenth-century politics in opposition to the Tories, and which was named after those who in the seventeenth century had sought to exclude the Roman Catholic James Stuart succeeding to the thrones of England, Scotland, and Ireland. But there was a darker side to this celebration of progress, as this progress had only been achieved at a terrible cost – the devastations and executions of the Reformation and Counter-Reformation, the carnage of the British and Irish Civil Wars, the exploitation of the labouring classes, and the creation of the slave trade. Progress was a bloody affair, so these guilty secrets were buried deep in the national consciousness – and yet emerged in the terror and horror of Gothic literature and art: history refused to stay buried, the past haunted the present.

Gothic literature gripped the imagination of the later eighteenth century, and in my book on *The Gothic* (2012) I argue that its defining feature is sublimity: the attempt to open the mind to the annihilating experience of the infinite. The key theorist here is Edmund Burke, whose *Philosophical Enquiry into the Origin of our Ideas of the Sublime and the Beautiful* (1757) argued – with terrific influence – that such sublimity was achieved through obscurity: obscurity that roused the imagination with the terrors of eternity and the infinite. Thus, the sublime became a fundamental constituent of a particularly Whig form of literature: aesthetics was decidedly not independent of party politics.

So, taking my cue from William Empson's *Seven Types of Ambiguity* (1930), I proposed 'seven types of obscurity' in my book to exemplify the Burkean sublime and Gothic aesthetics (Groom 2012, 77-8).

1. Meteorological obscurity (mists, clouds, wind, rain, storm, tempest, smoke, darkness, shadows, gloom).
2. Topographical obscurity (impenetrable forests, inaccessible mountains, chasms, gorges, deserts, blasted heaths, icefields, the boundless ocean).
3. Architectural obscurity (towers, prisons, castles covered in gargoyles and crenellations, abbeys and priories, tombs, crypts, dungeons, ruins, graveyards, mazes, secret passages, locked doors).
4. Material obscurity (masks, veils, disguises, billowing curtains, suits of armour, tapestries).
5. Textual obscurity (riddles, rumours, folklore, unreadable manuscripts and inscriptions, ellipses, broken texts, fragments, clotted language, polysyllabism, obscure dialect, inserted narratives, stories-within-stories).
6. Spiritual obscurity (religious mystery, allegory and symbolism, ritual, mysticism, freemasonry, magic and the occult, Satanism, witchcraft, summonings, damnation).
7. Psychological obscurity (dreams, visions, hallucinations, drugs, sleep-walking, madness, split personalities, mistaken identities, doubles, derangement, ghostly presences, forgetfulness, death, hauntings).

These forms of obscurity are nearly all instantly familiar in Tolkien's work, as I began to consider at the 2012 Tolkien Society Conference *The Return of the Ring* (Groom 2016).

1. Meteorological obscurity: instances in Tolkien would be, for example, the Misty Mountains, mist on the road to Bucklebury Ferry, fog on the Barrow-downs, Weathertop, the Great Darkness on the Pelennor Fields, the deluge that engulfs Númenor.
2. Topographical obscurity in Middle-earth includes Mirkwood and the Old Forest, Caradhras, the Dead Marshes (without the aid of Gollum), Thangorodrim, the Teiglin (where Glaurung was slain), the Uttermost West.
3. As for architectural obscurity, Middle-earth is littered with ancient and ruined architecture. There are many subterranean tunnels and passages, from Moria to the Paths of the Dead. Other examples include the dungeons of Dol Guldur, Barad-dûr, and Angband; as well as Minas Morgul, Orthanc, the Paths of the Dead, the Barrows, Shelob's Lair, the tunnels under the Misty Mountains, and so forth.
4. Material disguises range from the dark shrouds of the Black Riders to the Elven cloaks of Lothlórien, from Éowyn's disguise as Dernhelm to Frodo and Samwise dressing as Mordor Orcs, as well as Frodo travelling as 'Mr Underhill', Aragorn posing as Strider, the unfurling of Arwen's standard, Beren and Lúthien disguising themselves as a werewolf and a vampire bat. Incidentally, 'Beren and Lúthien' is perhaps the most conventionally 'Gothic' of Tolkien's texts – in addition to these supernatural disguises there is the lustrous

darkness of Lúthien's hair, the subterranean settings, lust, dismemberment, a mixed marriage, and mortality, as well as the extraordinary image of the earthbound Morgoth falling like an avalanche.

5. Textual obscurities are at the very heart of Tolkien's Middle-earth in invented and often untranslated languages, found manuscripts such as Thrór's Map and its moon runes, the prophetic song 'The King Beneath the Mountains' sung at Laketown, the inscription on the Ring, the manuscript of Isildur discovered by Gandalf, the mislaid letter at The Prancing Pony, Gandalf's enigmatic scratches on stone on Weathertop, and the Book of Mazarbul. History is governed by a prophecy concerning fragments ("Seek for the sword that was broken") that in turn motivates the Council of Elrond to decide on the fate of the One Ring, while the Witch-king Lord of the Nazgûl is protected by a foretelling that he shall not be slain by any living man – just two of the many riddles in Middle-earth, from the riddle-game of *The Hobbit* to the Gate of Moria (*FR*, 'The Council of Elrond', 322). More complex examples would be the unfinished and lost poems (not to mention 'Great Tales') in the legendarium, the different languages and dialects of Middle-earth, and the references in *The Lord of the Rings* not only to the First Age but also to Anglo-Saxon poetry and other historical sources – a reminder of Tolkien's philology that he claimed underpinned Middle-earth.

6. Spiritual mystery is a staple of Gothic fiction, but appears to offer less for the reader of Tolkien. Yet the spiritual is implicit – and suggestively understated – in half-acknowledged prayers in *The Lord of the Rings*: Sam's invocation when faced with Shelob is spoken

in a language he does not understand, while Faramir's contemplation of Númenor remains unexplained. There is certainly damnation, and forms of magic are exercised, as well as some limited attention to funeral rites such as Rohan's burial mounds – possibly derived from studies made by the eighteenth-century antiquarian William Stukeley (Hammond and Scull *Reader's Guide* 2006, 368). Yet even *The Silmarillion*, the 'Old Testament' of Middle-earth as Christopher Tolkien described it, does not offer much here – Númenor's tombs, the temple to Melkor, and ritual sacrifices being perhaps the prominent exceptions – but that is in part because immortals walk the earth. Moreover, magic is actually generally downplayed, although Sauron does shape-shift (notably in 'Beren and Lúthien'), characters such as Glaurung and Saruman have powers of bewitchment, and the Two Watchers are enchanted guardians of Cirith Ungol.

7. As to psychological issues, there are prophetic dreams, the visions that emerge from the Mirror of Galadriel and objects such as the *palantíri* (which also enslave users to the will of Sauron), the shifts in perception caused by the Ring, split identities (Gollum/Sméagol) and multi-named characters, doubles (the Nazgûl), derangement (the effects of the Ring on its bearers, wearers, and on contiguous characters such as Boromir), forgetfulness (Niënor), the distorted vision of Morgoth imposed on Húrin, and so on. There are monsters too: Smaug and other dragons, the Watcher in the Water, the Fell Beasts on which the Nazgûl ride, Shelob, and ghosts – the dead walk in the shape of Ringwraiths, Barrow-wights, and Oathbreakers.

Furthermore, the Shakespearian northern tragedies *Hamlet*, *King Lear*, and *Macbeth*, which themselves helped to inspire later Gothic literature, exert a strong influence on *The Lord of the Rings* (see Groom 2022b).

I'd like to say a little more about the disorientation of psychological states – in particular dreams – as the Gothic seems to be most prevalent here, creating alternative realities in Middle-earth as do the competing accounts of events in classic Gothic novels such as *Frankenstein* (1818), *Strange Case of Dr Jekyll and Mr Hyde* (1886), and *Dracula* (1897). The Hobbits dream almost constantly. At Buckland, Frodo dreams of a sea of trees, the sea, a white tower; in the Old Forest all four become drowsy and Sam dreams that he has been thrown into the River Withywindle by a tree. At the House of Tom Bombadil, Frodo has a vision of Gandalf on Orthanc, Pippin dreams of a willow tree, and Merry dreams of water. They are drowsy again on the Barrow-downs where the distances are "hazy and deceptive"; Frodo dreams and awakes in the Barrow; Merry dreams of the Barrow dead – memories of the Men of Carn Dûm become hauntingly present through the portals of standing stones (*FR*, 'Fog on the Barrow-downs', 187). Merry dreams again when he is overcome by the 'Black Breath' of the Riders at Bree, and Frodo dreams of a horn sounding and of galloping riders; Frodo, again, dreams of dark wings passing. The dreams continue at Rivendell, and in the Misty Mountains, and in Moria. Frodo's dreams then seem to coalesce in the Mirror of Galadriel: he sees a White Wizard, Bilbo (among his manuscripts, while rain beats against his window), the sea and ships, and the Eye. Lothlórien is like a dream. Sam wonders whether he is dreaming when thinks he sees Gollum on the River Anduin. Frodo has hyper-real visions on Amon Hen, the Seat of Seeing – yet seeing as through a "mist" (*FR*,

'The Breaking of the Fellowship', 519-20). Merry and Pippin's journey being marched by the Orcs is a "dark and troubled dream", repeatedly falling into "evil dreams" (*TT*, 'The Uruk-hai', 52, 57). Merry describes the movement of the Huorns as dreamlike – "I thought I was dreaming an Entish dream" – while Pippin has an almost Einsteinian dream of relativity when riding with Gandalf to Minas Tirith, as if "he and Gandalf were still as stone, seated upon the statue of a running horse, while the world rolled away beneath his feet" (*TT*, 'Flotsam and Jetsam', 211; 'The Palantír', 258). Frodo stares at the lights of the Dead Marshes as if in dream, and while on watch hallucinates between sleeping and waking; even Gollum has "secret dreams" (*TT*, 'Of Herbs and Stewed Rabbit', 319). Although their dreams in Ithilien are more peaceful, they quickly turn into nightmares. Shelob is revealed as "horrible beyond the horror of an evil dream", and Merry leaves the battlefield of the Pelennor Fields in a trance: "a meaningless journey in a hateful dream" (*TT*, 'Shelob's Lair', 420; *RK*, 'The Houses of Healing', 158). When Frodo hears Sam singing in the Tower of Cirith Ungol he of course thinks he is dreaming; later, in Mordor he dreams of fire, and is rescued from Mount Doom "in a dream" (*RK*, 'The Field of Cormallen', 276). Sam thinks that he has been dreaming until he sees Frodo's hand missing the third finger, and later, back in The Shire, declares it all "seems like a dream" – as does Merry (*RK*, 'The Grey Havens', 374). Not so for Frodo: for him, returning feels "more like falling asleep" (*RK*, 'Homeward Bound', 335).

When listed in this way, the sheer number of dreams the Hobbits dream – or believe they dream – is remarkable. The dreams create a continuous sense of unreality, of insecurity – especially concerning Frodo, who becomes indistinct, even spectral. These dreams are wholly individual and unshared experiences, emphasizing the isolation of characters – again, particularly Frodo. Humans dream too: Aragorn dreams of horses, Éowyn hears dark voices in dreams, and Faramir is not only feverish on his father's pyre but has a mystic dream that results in Boromir's pilgrimage to Rivendell as well as a recurring vision of the downfall of Númenor. For the people of Minas Tirith, the coming of the king is like a communal reverie – to be cherished, if also to be doubted – but for the Host of the West, the march to the Black Gate is a "hideous dream" and Mordor is a ghastly delirium (*RK*, 'The Black Gate Opens', 194). Collective nightmares such as this challenge the fabric of reality, while also suggesting the impossibility of representing what is real.

It appears, then, that Middle-earth is steeped in the Gothic, and that volumes and volumes could be written on Tolkien and the Gothic, on how to make sense of a world acknowledged as broken, imperfect, and inhospitable. Even before the final volume, *The Return of the King*, was published on 20 October 1955, the writer and reviewer Harvey Breit had interviewed Tolkien (by letter) for a piece in the *New York Times Book Review*, which was published on 5 June 1955 – although as Wayne Hammond and Christina Scull put it, the article "misleadingly convert[ed] Tolkien's terse answers into a continuous text" (Hammond and Scull *Chronology* 2006, 478).[2] From the beginning, the piece is a stark contrast between Breit's breeziness and Tolkien's irascibility:

How does it happen [asks Breit] that a writer of children's books (who began that way, if we may believe his critics) can end by producing a somber and brilliantly bizarre trilogy

---

2. Amended from earlier version: see https://www.hammondandscull.com/addenda/chronology_by_date.html

like 'The Lord of the Rings' – part two of which ('The Two Towers') was reviewed here recently and labeled definitely for adults? The author of that Gothic masterpiece, J.R.R. Tolkien, was asked how it all came about. What, we asked Dr. Tolkien makes you tick? Dr. T. [sic], who teaches at Oxford when he isn't writing novels, has this brisk reply: 'I don't tick. I am not a machine. (If I did tick, I should have no views on it, and you had better ask the winder.)' (Breit 1955, 8)

Having received the short article, Tolkien wrote to Paul Brooks on 10 June 1955, objecting, in the summary by Hammond and Scull, to Breit's "use of the word 'Gothic' [...] which in its literary sense represents an air Tolkien has tried to avoid" (Hammond and Scull *Chronology* 2006, 482; *Letters*, Letter 165, 217-21).

The statement seems unequivocal: Tolkien deliberately tried to avoid the Gothic in its literary sense – despite the recently reviewed *Two Towers* that included the passage of the Dead Marshes and the confrontation with Shelob, while the Paths of the Dead and the passage of Mordor was shortly to come in *The Return of the King*. Tolkien does refer to Stevenson's *Jekyll and Hyde* in a letter to Sir Stanley Unwin on 21 September 1947, describing the impossibility of combining his professional work with finishing *The Lord of the Rings*: "Hyde (or Jekyll) has had to have his way, and I have been obliged to devote myself mainly to philology"; he also refers to the ghost stories of M.R. James in the notes to his lecture 'On Fairy-stories' (*Letters*, Letter 111, 124; *OFS*, 261, 299).[3] But there are no references in his published work (as far as I know) to *Frankenstein*, *Dracula*, or comparable Gothic literature.[4]

---

3. See Cilli 274 (item 2200), 132 (items 1092, 1093).
4. The papers by Victoria Holtz and Stephen Brehe from *Tolkien and the Gothic* (2022) are nevertheless thought-provoking.

The reason for Tolkien's antipathy towards Gothic literature – despite the proliferation of Gothic imagery and motifs – is, I think, primarily one of nomenclature: none of this, for Tolkien, is properly Gothic – rather, it is the dark end of fantasy or fairy tale. The Gothic meant something very different to Tolkien. For a start, Tolkien's intellectual life was literally located in the Gothic – or at least in the Gothic Revival. In 1900, he passed the entrance exam to King Edward's School, then housed in an imposing Gothic Revival building designed by Charles Barry, the architect responsible for the Palace of Westminster, which had been rebuilt in the three decades following 1840.[5] Exeter College, Oxford, where Tolkien studied as an undergraduate, had a fine new nineteenth-century chapel built in the decorated Gothic style and modelled on Sainte Chappelle, and the Oxford Oratory where he regularly attended mass was another Gothic Revival building – as was Leeds University, where Tolkien's professional academic life began in 1921.

But even this more edifying understanding of the Gothic and its associations with learning and faith does not get to the heart of Tolkien's Gothic. Tolkien discovered the ancient Gothic language in 1908 or 1909 via Joseph Wright's *Primer of the Gothic Language*. Little of Gothic survives – there is, for instance, no poetry – but it nevertheless stirred in him "a sensation at least as full of delight as [that of John Keats] first looking into Chapman's *Homer*" (*Monsters*, 192).[6] Tolkien also found the Gothic script beautiful, and enjoyed writing Gothicized inscriptions; and, undaunted by the lost vocabulary and literary culture, he simply invented missing Gothic words and ultimately wrote his own Gothic poetry – notably 'Bagmē

---

5. Sadly, Barry's building was demolished in the 1930s.
6. The allusion is to John Keats's sonnet that describes his first reading of George Chapman's translations of the *Odyssey* and the *Iliad*.

Blōma', eventually published in *Songs for the Philologists*.[7]
When he took up his place at Oxford in 1911, he was tutored
in Comparative Philology by Joseph Wright – the same Wright
who had written the *Gothic Primer* that had so enthralled him.

Here we approach the heart of Tolkien's Gothic: the ancient
Germanic people who spoke and wrote in a beautiful, now lost,
language. Gothic, he wrote, "was the first to take me by storm,
to move my heart" (*Monsters*, 191-2). Early in his academic
career in a translation of *Beowulf* made while at the University
of Leeds, Tolkien equated the Geats of *Beowulf* with the Goths,
and lectured on 'Legends of the Goths'. They became woven
into his mythology: many commentators have pointed out that
the people of Rhovanion have Gothic names – in particular, the
names of the Rohirrim chieftains before the Eorl dynasty are
Gothic – and there was a tradition that 'Goths' meant 'Horse-
folk', just as Hengist and Horsa were the 'horse lords'. So the
Rohirrim are not simply reinvented equestrian Anglo-Saxons,
but essentially Goths, and Tom Shippey argues that the Battle
of Pelennor Fields is based on the Battle of the Catalaunian
Plains fought in AD451 between the Romans and the Visigoths
against the Huns supported by the Ostrogoths (Shippey 2005,
18).[8] Names in *The Lost Road* are also taken from the Gothic,

---

7. See the paper by Mahdî Brecq in the present volume.
8. Sandra Ballif Straubhaar goes so far as to argue that the marriage of
Faramir to Éowyn is reminiscent of dynastic marriages between Romans and
Goths in late antiquity. Shippey further connects Gondor and classical Rome
in decline, claiming that against the Riders of Rohan, "Gondor is a kind of
Rome" (2005, 149). But this does not fit either the Gothic paradigm or the
history of Middle-earth at the end of the Third Age: Rome of course fell to
the Goths, and a newly risen Rome would not have made Gothic culture
sustainable. In contrast, Kathleen Herbert suggests that the incursions of the
Orcs are reminiscent of accounts of invading Huns (1993, 271, 225); see
also Dimitra Fimi, who draws attention to Tolkien's revealingly conflicting
attempts to theorize Orcs (2010, 155). But in any case, these critics ignore the

and the associated poem 'King Sheave' is a Gothic myth. Most explicitly, *The Legend of Sigurd and Gudrún* assimilates the Gothic narrative poem incorporated into *Heiðreks saga ins vitra*, 'The Battle of the Goths and Huns' (Shippey 2010, 308-14).

Moreover, in an unpublished lecture, 'The Goths', Tolkien wrote:

> In vain we regret the past, or speculate on what might have been. Yet it is inevitable that we should regret. […] In dealing with the Goths – regret cannot be avoided, if not regret for what might have been, at any rate regret for our altogether scanty records of what was […] the vanishing of their tradition, literature, history, and most of their tongue. (Hammond and Scull Reader's Guide 2006, 555)

So rather than seeing the Goths as the barbarians who had brought about the collapse of the Roman Empire, Tolkien argued that the Romans had brought about "the ruin of Gaul and the submergence of its native language (or languages) arts and traditions […] dooming to obscurity and debate the history of perhaps the most remarkable of the Cymric speaking peoples" (555).

These true Gothic influences emerge with quiet insistence in Middle-earth. In *The Hobbit*, for instance, Thorin refers to the Dwarves and himself as the heirs of Durin, the "father of the fathers of the eldest race of Dwarves", which reaffirms the legendarium as a key frame of reference here (Anderson 2002, 96, 98; *Letters*, Letter 25, 30-2; see Rateliff, ii. 855-65). But Thorin also calls the Dwarves 'Longbeards', making them part of north European Gothic antiquity by hinting at a connection

---

Catholic dimensions of the Gothic myth that are discussed below.

with the Lombards, known in Anglo-Saxon as *Longbeardan*. The 'Longbeards' were, moreover, not only an element of the mythic matter of England surveyed in mediaeval Gothic histories, but were also woven into Tolkien's abandoned novel *The Lost Road* (*Lost Road*, 53).The Dwarves were, in other words, crypto-Goths.

Most extraordinarily, the linguistic essay 'The Languages and Peoples of the Third Age' (Appendix F of *The Lord of the Rings*) includes a section on translation, in which Tolkien 'admits' to having translated the proper nouns of his story from Westron (the 'Common Speech') into a more familiar English idiom: he has, in other words, 'Englished' all the names (*RK*, 'Appendix F', 525; see Hiley 2015). So The Shire is not really The Shire, but *Sûza*; Sam (short for Samwise, from the Anglo-Saxon *samwîs*) is not really Sam but *Banazîr*, and Gamgee is really *Galbasi* – all words based on the Gothic language: Gothic is the linguistic medium of Middle-earth. So Hobbits are crypto-Goths as well. In the final pages of *The Lord of the Rings*, then, Tolkien completely inverts the reader's experience of The Shire, Sam, everything by revealing the alien unfamiliarity of what for nigh-on fifteen hundred pages has become recognizably familiar. It is a stunning, almost literal *mise-en-abîme*: a sudden and infinite regress. Middle-earth is, it transpires, unreachably remote after all and abruptly recedes into the primal *uncanniness* of a mysterious lost language.

The Gothic, then for Tolkien, is not the Gothic novel or even mediaeval architecture, but a lost language of antiquity – and Middle-earth attempts the impossible by, in part, trying to recreate it. But I would like to pause a moment on my introduction of the word *uncanniness*. Sigmund Freud's paper 'The "Uncanny"' was published in 1919; it has subsequently been developed by many critics – particularly in the field of Gothic studies. For Freud, the 'Uncanny' is the familiar made unfamiliar – the homely made unhomely – although these meanings also merge the familiar with the unfamiliar to make it strangely familiar: something unhomely at the heart of the homely.[9] Hence the 'Uncanny' is uncertain, ambiguous – and creates uncertainty, ambiguity, and misinterpretation. The 'Uncanny' therefore emerges as an effect rather than an inherent property of literary works. There is no such thing as an 'Uncanny' novel, and although a novel may have 'Uncanny' episodes, these may differ for different readers and at different times. The 'Uncanny' is consequently part of the reading experience, unsettling the ways in which we read. In this way, the 'Uncanny' is part of one's subjective response to a text, and so troubles one's own personal identity through reading.

For Freud, the 'Uncanny' can manifest through repetition (including doubles), coincidences, animism, automatism, uncertainty about gender and sexuality, live burial, telepathy and magical powers, severed limbs (or heads or eyes), solitude (or silence or darkness), and death. These elements have been thoroughly discussed and dissected by later critics, who have also noted the absence of history in Freud's analysis, his emphasis on examples from literature rather than other arts, and the likely influence on his thinking of the traumas of isolation and identity crises triggered by the Great War (see Royle 2003; Bartholomew 2019).

Freud's essay begins with six pages of dictionary definitions and etymologies before proceeding circuitously via unexpected byways and idiosyncratic digressions – much as Tolkien does in his own academic essays – and Freud's identifications of the 'Uncanny' are indeed very suggestive for readers of Tolkien.

---

9. See Sofia Skeva's paper in the present volume.

One could find scores of examples of potentially 'Uncanny' moments in Tolkien's writings – not least, in the significance of home and homeliness in both *The Hobbit* and *The Lord of the Rings*. Hobbits seldom forget home, and of course at the end of *The Lord of the Rings* are faced with a devastating reckoning with their own homeland; Frodo, however, can never return home himself and is forever estranged from Middle-earth – othered – eventually only able to find some sort of peace in that most alien of places, Valinor. Many of the examples already outlined in discussing the sublime have 'Uncanny' resonances – particularly in *The Lord of the Rings*. Clearly there is much repetition and doubling, coincidence and/or fate, the animism and automatism of the Ring, thought transference and communion, sorcery, isolation and estrangement, and so forth. But it is not enough simply to catalogue these 'Uncanny' instances. Why does *The Lord of the Rings* abound with 'Uncanniness' – and is it really 'Uncanny'?

The answer lies less, I think, with Freudian psychoanalysis and more with English history. Tolkien challenges the English Protestant Whig model of history that had held sway throughout much of the eighteenth and nineteenth centuries from an 'Uncanny' perspective. Gothic was Whiggish, which not only meant it was parliamentarian but also Protestant and thereby profoundly anti-Catholic. Indeed, the English Reformation was declared to be a repeat of the original fifth-century Gothic rebellion against Roman tyranny, this time standing against the Roman Catholic Church as opposed to Imperial Rome. The signal moments in the march of progress were watersheds when individual freedoms were supposedly extended – often at the cost of religious persecution: the signing of Magna Carta, the Reformation and the thwarting of the Counter-Reformation, and the 'Glorious Revolution' – the accession to the throne of the Dutch Protestant William of Orange, after which the Act of Settlement (1701) ensured that succession to the throne would remain exclusively Protestant.[10] That was the Whig basis of history.

I have written previously that Tolkien, as a Catholic, wrote "as an active mediaevalist [...] purposely to reconnect with and revive mediaeval identities" (Groom 2016, 33). Previously, I argued that Tolkien could be seen in a tradition of specifically Catholic Gothicists – there is even a covert Jacobitism in his depiction of kings and sovereignty.[11] Richard Verstegan, for instance, whose *A Restitution of Decayed Intelligence in Antiquities* was published in 1605, attempted to restore Germanic national origins and aboriginal Catholicism to the English through arguments based on a combination of both philological and legendary evidence. The parallels with Tolkien are striking: Verstegan reinvented the Goths through ethnographic and etymological evidence, made Hengist and Horsa the founders of England, and entrusted the 'English-Saxon' tongue as the deliverer of national character.

Similarly, Tolkien's focus was ever on 'peoples, not races'. As he argued in his lecture 'English and Welsh', "We are dealing with events that are primarily a struggle between languages" (*Monsters*, 167). So Verstegan's fascination with identity and

---

10. With regard to Milton, as Debbie Sly points out, "Paradoxically, what Tolkien and Milton have most in common as artists, their devout Christianity, also divides them: Milton rewrites Genesis from a radically Protestant and Renaissance perspective, whereas Tolkien's Roman Catholicism inspires a version of the universe that is at times distinctly medieval, although it also reflects the cataclysmic events of the twentieth century" (Sly 2000, 107).

11. Tolkien's Catholic Gothicism even suggests a covert Jacobitism to kings and to sovereignty (see Groom 2022, 74, 138). Although Tolkien suggested various different titles for the volumes, *The Return of the King* was mooted from the outset – it is surely too much to be a coincidence.

its relationship to heritage and landscape origins was a legacy embraced by Tolkien. Consistent with later eighteenth-century thinking, a people was defined by language and the culture which the language generated and gradually developed, not by its racial origins and purity:

> For though cultural and other traditions may accompany a difference of language, they are chiefly maintained and preserved by language. Language is the prime differentiator of people – not of 'races', whatever that much-misused word may mean in the long-blended history of western Europe. (166)

He goes on to celebrate the "racially [...] mixed invaders" of Britain – a favourite theme of English antiquarianism (171).

For Tolkien, as for Verstegan (and also for the eighth-century monk the Venerable Bede, and the Victorian architect Augustus Welby Pugin too), the Goths were the primal Germanic Catholics, an alternative to classical paganism, and to Protestantism. The Gothic language had, Tolkien believed, "reached the eminence of liturgical use, but failed owing to the tragic history of the Goths to become one of the liturgical languages of the West" – the unfortunate consequence of their adherence to the Arian heresy, or disputing the divinity of Christ. Robert Murray, remembered that in August 1973:

> Ronald was maintaining with great vigour over the luncheon table that one of the greatest disasters of European history was the fact that the Goths turned Arian: but for that, their languages, just ready to become classical, would have been enriched not only with a great bible version but also, on Byzantine principles, with a vernacular liturgy, which would

have served as a model for all the Germanic peoples and would have given them a native Catholicism which would never break apart. And with that he rose and in splendidly sonorous tones declaimed the Our Father in Gothic. (Hammond and Scull *Chronology* 2006, 773)

The 'Our Father' in Gothic begins,

Atta unsar þu in himinam weihnai namo þein·
qimai þiudinassus þeins· wairþai wilja þeins·
swe in himina jah ana airþai· (Miller 2019, 476)

It is one of the very few extant Gothic texts (Evans 2002, 199). The poverty of the Gothic literary and linguistic tradition was symptomatic of the tragedy of history – as Tolkien wrote shortly after the publication of *The Return of the King*: "I am […] a Roman Catholic, so that I do not expect 'history' to be anything but a 'long defeat' – though it contains (and in a legend may contain more clearly and movingly) some examples or glimpses of final victory" (*Letters*, Letter 195, 255). The 'long defeat' repeats the haunting phrase used by Galadriel: "together through the ages of the world we have fought the long defeat" – the Elves too being, perhaps, crypto-Goths (*FR*, 'The Mirror of Galadriel', 463). The phrase the 'long defeat' thus binds together the Goths, the dissolution of English Catholicism, and the disenchantment of Middle-earth.

But if this is Tolkien's Gothic, it is a radical departure from canonical Gothic literature. However, I would now like to propose that his Gothicism is more subtle. For Tolkien, history is disappointment, it is failure, it is loss: it is neither Whiggishly progressive nor Modernistically technological, and he actually turns the expectations of progress and improvement upside down. Tolkien had already commenced on his lifelong legendarium three years before Freud's essay was published, and while the Great War certainly spelt the end for the Whig theory of history – not least as things continued to decline catastrophically in the ensuing uneasy peace – it also presented Tolkien with an opportunity to consider an alternative Catholic history. He deploys similar tropes to Freud, but as part of an audacious historical hypothesis: that English history is misbegotten and therefore deeply suspect. Heretofore, Tolkien proposes, history has been bastardized, illegitimate: the history of Middle-earth – and especially *The Lord of the Rings* – accordingly revises assumptions about English history to make the familiar unfamiliar, from the 'Great Tales' of the First Age, which all end in defeat, to more singular examples, such as 'the return of the king' at the end of the Third Age.[12]

The 'Uncanniness' in so much of the novel defamiliarizes and so questions the triumphalism of English history. This is one reason why the novel has been neglected – even dismissed – by the self-proclaimed cognoscenti of English literary criticism. They fail to see how radically challenging it is, and – lacking a sufficiently broad frame of historical reference – dismiss it. But the more one learns about the mysterious movements of English history, the more 'Uncanny' *The Lord of the Rings* becomes in relation to that history and way of thinking.

And yet at the same time one wonders how relevant Freud's 'Uncanny' really is today. It is not so much the unfamiliar within the familiar (as the late radical philosopher Mark Fisher put it), as the *all-too familiar* within the familiar (Fisher 2016, 8-13). Take Freud's list. First, repetition and doubles: we are

---

12. The king, Elessar, returns as a Catholic Stuart, and, not unlike Charles II, Aragorn has also been wandering in exile – or 'on his travels', as eighteenth-century Jacobites put it – as Strider.

in an insistently repetitive society that has been accelerating in repetition for at least the past half-century. Although books have been read and reread for centuries, the experience (beyond childhood books) is different each time; however, the repetition of recorded music has literally become the soundtrack of our lives. This ranges from intentional repetition by listening to one's own digital playlists, to unavoidably hearing background music in supermarkets or while on hold to a call centre. Repeatedly watching a film only used to be possible by returning to the cinema during its initial release; but then there were repeats on television, then videotapes, and now DVDs. So too television – children growing up today repeatedly ask to see exactly the same episode of a series over and over again. We ourselves have also become not only doubled but multiplied thousands of times through digital photography and are wholly familiar with our photographic and video selves – as have Tolkien's characters through films, computer games, and merchandizing.

Likewise, coincidence – the most extraordinary coincidences are now everyday occurrences because of the global news network. The same numbers being drawn for a national lottery in successive weeks is not only entirely imaginable, but happened in Bulgaria in 2009, with the same numbers being drawn twice in five days. Similarly, several people have won lottery jackpots more than once with the same numbers. And it is not only the reporting of global news stories that familiarizes us to such coincidences, it is also the huge proliferation of lotteries around the world.

Animism and automatism too. Computer-generated imagery can bring anything imaginable to life, from sentient cuddly toys to alien invasions on a planetary scale. CGI is now the movie industry standard and is taught in UK schools from about the age of ten, as well as being a teaching device in its own right.

So we have become acclimatized to living in worlds that are simultaneously real and unreal, accessing experience and information through screens. Much as the plough extended the productive capacities of agricultural workers but also separated them a little from the land, so mobile phones extend our voices and images to an international audience while simultaneously dislocating us from our listeners. There is no longer anything uncanny about hearing a disembodied voice from thousands of miles away (or indeed from decades ago). Our reality has very quickly adapted to digital communication media, and barely notices that it is a form of telepathy or technological magic – as are such things as flight, the internet, keyhole surgery, and artificial intelligence. Reassessments of gender and sexuality are political issues and international events through Pride Month. That just leaves solitude, severed limbs (and heads and eyes), live burial, and death. Solitude and, figuratively speaking, live burial were part of the routine lockdown experience for many, but I will allow that dismembered bodies and probably death as well remain somewhat uncanny in the Freudian sense.

The point of this is to suggest an alternative term for this new intimacy with what was once so outré as to be uncanny: the *eldritch* – the final definition of *eldritch* in the *OED* being 'Weird, ghostly, unnatural, frightful, hideous'. Mobile phones and digital media are not uncanny, but their familiar and relaxed wondrousness is *eldritch* – they bring the supernatural into daily lives in the most convenient of ways. Now, there are obviously no mobile phones or digital media in Middle-earth – but there are *palantíri* and visions of other worlds. The *palantíri* are rapidly accepted and are irresistibly attractive to an 'early adopter' such as Pippin, who does what nearly every geek does when they get a new gadget which is to fire it up without reading the instruction manual and in doing so crashes the programme. As to visions, the Ring (as well as the Mirror of Galadriel) create other worlds: Frodo sees and hears the Ringwraiths in new ways when he is wearing the Ring during their attack at Weathertop, or gazing at the teeming landscape from the Seat of Seeing on Amon Hen.

While I am being slightly frivolous here, I would nevertheless say that at times Tolkien's work seems strikingly prescient. But the point is how readily characters adapt to new objects and situations. Aragorn, for example, swiftly weaponizes the *palantír*, while Frodo, although keenly possessive of the Ring (like Bilbo), barely contemplates it once Gandalf has given him its history, and Bilbo only asks to see it once when Frodo arrives at Rivendell; similarly, characters such as Boromir propose weaponizing the Ring and using it against Sauron. My point is that the *palantíri* and the Ring are quickly accepted: they are eldritch rather than uncanny. Now, I know that the Ring in particular is a highly complex object or entity, but rather than be distracted by details, I am suggesting using these objects in order to move to a much more significant point: how rapidly readers accept the unfamiliarity of Middle-earth, particularly its peoples, and especially its different species. *Species*, not races (Groom 2022, xiv, 305-6). The various species of Middle-earth – Elves, Ents, Dwarves, Hobbits, Humans, Orcs – are unhesitatingly accepted by readers: this is no 'Uncanny Valley'. Yes, there are a few moments of strangeness – such as when Elrond admits to having been the herald of Gil-galad and present at the Battle of the Last Alliance over three thousand years before, but one of the ways in which the book works and succeeds brilliantly is by destabilizing a Human-centred perception with new ways of seeing; this perspective is most apparent in Tolkien's repeated emphasis on non-Human species and is key to understanding Middle-earth today.

In addition to the ever-present characterization of non-Human species, Tolkien also draws the reader into non-Human perspectives, into new sensitivities and insights. Gimli provides several moments of 'Dwarrowcentric' thinking in his love of rocks, caves, and the subterranean. Tolkien describes the Glittering Caves, but then invites the reader to perceive them with both Dwarvish and Elvish eyes – Dwarrowcentric and Alvocentric perceptions, respectively – the latter having no language for the husbandry and cultivation of stone.[13] Gimli's rock-solid sense of selfhood and being is then shattered in the remarkable passage when he enters the Paths of the Dead and the reader enters his mind: he becomes 'lithophobic', terrified of stones. The Dwarf should literally be in his element under the mountain, but his mind splinters "and at once a blindness came upon him, even upon Gimli Glóin's son who had walked unafraid in many deep places of the world" (*RK*, 'The Passing of the Grey Company', 65). This is Dwarrowcentric dread, a horror experienced by a Dwarvish – a non-Human – consciousness, that leaves Gimli "crawling like a beast" before he escapes "in some other world" (67). Similarly, Treebeard gives an Entish account of Middle-earth – essentially the view from the trees, where time and space function differently, where identity (the individual Ent) and the community (the forest) coexist – a sensibility that cries out for trees to be given rights (Curry 2004, 48-86, 155; Macfarlane 2019). As the 'geologian' (or Christian environmentalist philosopher) Thomas Berry puts it in *The Great Work*,

> every being has rights to be recognized and revered. Trees have tree rights, insects have insect rights, rivers have river rights, mountains have mountain rights. (Berry 1999, 5)

---

13. 'Alvocentric': derived from the Middle English *alve*, meaning Elf.

Tolkien therefore helps to normalize non-anthropocentric (Human-centred) narratives, which had already been developing in works from Anna Sewell's *Black Beauty* (1877) to George Orwell's *Animal Farm* (1945), and even in Franz Kafka's *Metamorphosis* (1915, translated 1933). *The Lord of the Rings*, however, is quite different: it is neither a children's book nor a political allegory nor a grotesque Expressionist novella, yet the text abounds in non-anthropocentric capacities of an arresting range and complexity, and through all the labyrinthine intricacies of his legendarium Tolkien mobilizes 'Otherness' on every page. These alternative viewpoints do not simply cover the various species of Elves, Dwarves, Hobbits, and so forth, but include a pensive fox and a soar of giant eagles, yammering spiders and evil things "in spider-form", trees and running water, and objects such as the One Ring and the *palantíri* (*TT*, 'Shelob's Lair', 417). Most explicitly, Aragorn describes the Black Riders as living in a different world of sensory experience (anticipating Thomas Nagel in his pioneering essay, 'What Is It Like To Be A Bat?'): "They themselves do not see the world of light as we do, but our shapes cast shadows in their minds, which only the noon sun destroys"; however, "in the dark they perceive many signs and forms that are hidden from us" and "at all times they smell the blood of living things" and also feel their presence: "Senses, too, there are other than sight or smell", and their horses can see for them (*FR*, 'A Knife in the Dark', 255).

When we read Tolkien, then, we should never forget that we are persistently being presented with non-Human perspectives, and this is in part where the popularity of the books lies (although few perhaps recognize it): in the ludic, the playfulness, and the permission to become Other.[14] This is a sentient world in which Humanity and Human perspectives form only a part, and which also looks forward to focusing on the non-Human. The philosopher Zygmunt Bauman argues that we should be "restoring to the world what modernity, presumptuously, had taken away; as a re-*enchantment* of artifice that has been dismantled; the modern conceit of meaning – the world that modernity tried hard to *disenchant*" – a form, then, of post-modernity (Bauman 1992, x; Curry 2004, 13). Such 'enchantment' is key to understanding Tolkien's fascination with fairy stories, and, in combining multiple non-Human and object-centred viewpoints, his work can offer a refreshingly positive perspectives on current crises (*OFS*, 59-66). In a comparable way, in his environmental study *The Song of the Earth* Jonathan Bate maintains that,

> we cannot do without thought-experiments and language-experiments which imagine a return to nature, a reintegration of the human and the Other. [...] [O]ur survival as a species may be dependent on our capacity to dream it in the work of our imagination. (2000, 37-8; Buell 2005, 107)

Ultimately, this flexible thinking can offer a far more positive way of delineating the Human and engage with the urgent challenges that currently confront us – which is the premise of my book *Twenty-First-Century Tolkien*. The disparate elements in Tolkien's Gothic, acknowledged and unacknowledged, thus combine to create the distinctly un-Gothic prospect of envisioning hope through the extinction of enchantment: a eucatastophe that is the very antithesis of conventional Gothic.

---

14. This may also account for the deliberate assuming of names, costumes, and masks at conventions: it is healthy role-play.

Bibliography

Anderson, Douglas A. (ed.), J.R.R. Tolkien, *The Annotated Hobbit: Revised and Expanded Edition,* (New York: Houghton Mifflin, 2002).

Bartholomew, H.G., 'Enstranged Strangers: OOO, the Uncanny, and the Gothic', *Open Philosophy,* 2 (2019), 357-83.

Bate, Jonathan, *The Song of the Earth,* (London: Picador: 2000).

Bauman, Zygmunt, *Intimations of Postmodernity,* (London and New York: Routledge, 1992).

Berry, Thomas, *The Great Work: Our Way Back into the Future,* (Bell Tower: New York, 1999).

Breit, Harvey, 'Oxford Calling', *New York Times Book Review* (June 5, 1955), 8.

Buell, Lawrence, *The Future of Environmental Criticism: Environmental Crisis and Literary Imagination,* (Malden, MA, Oxford, and Carlton, Vic.: Blackwell Publishing, 2005).

Curry, Patrick, *Defending Middle-earth: Myth and Modernity,* (Boston and New York: Houghton Mifflin, 2004).

Evans, Jonathan, 'The Anthropology of Arda: Creation, Theology, and the Race of Men', in Jane Chance (ed.), *Tolkien the Medievalist,* (London and New York: Routledge, 2002), pp. 194-224.

Fisher, Mark, *The Weird and The Eerie,* (London: Repeater Books, 2016).

Fimi, Dimitra, *Tolkien, Race and Cultural History: From Fairies to Hobbits,* (Houndmills: Palgrave Macmillan, 2010).

Freud, Sigmund, 'The "Uncanny"', in *The Standard Edition of Complete Psychological Works of Sigmund Freud*, 24 vols, ed. James Strachey, with Anna Freud, Alix Strachey, and Alan Tyson (London: Hogarth Press, 1953-74): vol. 17, *An Infantile Neurosis and Other Works,* (1917-1919), pp. 218-52.

Groom, Nick, 'The English Literary Tradition: Shakespeare to the Gothic', *A Companion to J.R.R. Tolkien*, ed. by Stuart D. Lee, second edition (Hoboken, NJ and Chichester: Wiley Blackwell, 2022), pp. 283-96.

—, *The Gothic: A Very Short Introduction,* (Oxford: Oxford University Press, 2012).

—, 'Tolkien and the Gothic', *The Return of the Ring: Proceedings of the Tolkien Society Conference 2012*, ed. by Lynn Forest-Hill, 2 vols (Edinburgh: Luna Press Publishing, 2016), ii, pp. 25-34.

—, *Twenty-First-Century Tolkien: What Middle-Earth Means To Us Today*, new edn (London: Atlantic, 2023).

Hammond, Wayne G. and Christina Scull (eds), *The J. R. R. Tolkien Companion & Guide*, 2 vols (Boston and New York: Houghton Mifflin, 2006).

Herbert, Kathleen, *Spellcraft: Old English Heroic Legends,* (Pinner: Anglo-Saxon Books, 1993).

Macfarlane, Robert, 'Should this tree have the same rights as you?': https://www.theguardian.com/books/2019/nov/02/trees-have-rights-too-robert-macfarlane-on-the-new-laws-of-nature

Miller, D. Gary, *The Oxford Gothic Grammar,* (Oxford: Oxford University Press, 2019).

Royle, Nicholas, *The Uncanny,* (Manchester University Press, 2003).

Shippey, Tom, *The Road to Middle-earth*, revised edn (London: Harper Collins, 2005).

—, *Tolkien: Author of the Century,* (London: HarperCollins, 2000).

—, 'Tolkien's Reconstruction of the Legends of *Sigurd and Gudrún*', *Tolkien Studies,* 7 (2010), 291-324.

Sly, Debbie, 'Weaving Nets of Gloom: "Darkness Profound" in Tolkien and Milton', in George Clark and Daniel Timmons, *J.R.R. Tolkien and His Literary Resonances: Views of Middle-earth,* (Westport, CT: Greenwood Press, 2000), pp. 109-19.

Straubhaar, Sandra Ballif, 'Myth, Late Roman History, and Multiculturalism in Tolkien's Middle-earth', in Jane Chance (ed.), *Tolkien and the Invention of Myth: A Reader,* (Lexington: University Press of Kentucky, 2004), pp. 101-17.

Tolkien, J.R.R., *The Lord of the Rings*, 3 vols, 3rd edn (London, Boston, and Sydney: Unwin Paperbacks, 1979).

—— *The Monsters and the Critics and Other Essays*, ed. by Christopher Tolkien (London: HarperCollins, 2006).

—— *The Letters of J.R.R. Tolkien*, ed. by Humphrey Carpenter with the assistance of Christopher Tolkien (London: HarperCollins, 2006).

—— *Tolkien On Fairy-stories: Expanded Edition, with Commentary and Notes*, ed. by Verlyn Flieger and Douglas A. Anderson (London: HarperCollins, 2014).

(Re-)Writing the (Monstrous) Body in 20th Century Fantasy Literature: The Construction of the Stranger in J.R.R. Tolkien's *The Lord of the Rings*

Sofia Skeva

In her discussion of the Gothic in terms of chronology, Emma McEvoy stresses the importance of exploring "the development and adaptation" of certain recurring Gothic motifs (2007, 7). These might include "set characters and typical plots", tropes, repeated motifs that are encountered through Gothic literary texts (7). Then again, despite the persistence of certain motifs and structural relations, Gothic appears to continuously reinvent itself (7). It is very interesting to consider, at this point, the construction of new possibilities within the Gothic as we attempt to situate it in terms of history and trace certain Gothic conventions and how they are displayed or transformed within a text in relation to its historical context. Taking into consideration early manifestations of the Gothic monster in literature, the current paper will seek to examine the way the latter has come to function within J.R.R. Tolkien's *The Lord of the Rings* (1954-1955). Specifically, the current paper argues that by projecting the Gothic monster and what it essentially represents onto the figure of the stranger Tolkien's literary text propagates an essentialist approach to cultural difference. By determining who can be assimilated in the Western home-space Tolkien defines (national) identity in terms of frontiers. Under this scope, the Gothic monster is transformed to illustrate "the unassimilable other", the strange being that enables us to "face the 'limit' of the multicultural nation" (Ahmed 2000, 106). In this context, it becomes apparent that, despite appearing culturally inclusive, Tolkien's fantasy world replicates values linked to imperialist ideologies with both monstrosity and otherness deeply racialized, signifying the "outsider", or the stranger whose stereotypical evil nature is prominent within the exploration of the secondary world while its proximity is deemed threatening to the well-being of the collective (national) home-space.

From classical times through to the Renaissance, monsters signified signs of divine anger or indications of forthcoming disasters with those monsters being basically constructed out of disproportionate, mismatched parts (like the griffin), or "grotesquely excessive" (like the hydra) or even incomplete, lacking essential body parts (Punter and Byron 2004, 263). By the eighteenth century, however, the dreadful appearance of the monster had begun to gradually change, illustrating in turn an increasingly moral function (263). Taken a step further, the notion of the Gothic monster as one that essentially encapsulates and displays societal fears and moral preoccupations first emerges in the 19th century following the publication of Mary Shelley's *Frankenstein* (1818). What appears then to be primarily important for the Gothic is the cultural function of the monster as it constructs the boundaries of normality through its difference in appearance or behavior suggesting at the same time the boundaries of what is experienced as "human" (263). By providing or even challenging those limits, Gothic texts repeatedly draw attention to the very nature of the monster, how it is imagined to signify the other and the way it is positioned as innately evil or inferior within the literary text.

As in the case of Frankenstein the exploration of the supposed imaginary lines between life and death and the going beyond the 'humanly possible' to create new life is what essentially triggers the 'monstrous' results to emerge. As David Punter and Glennis Byron point out "[l]imits and boundaries can therefore be reinstated as the monster is dispatched, good is distinguished from evil and self from other" (2004, 264).

The domestication of Gothic figures, monsters, spaces, and themes during the Victorian era provides another dimension as the horrors of the Gothic become realized and located within the world of the reader. The mythological monsters, and the image of the Gothic villain become transformed as supernatural entities, griffins, ghosts, monks, bandits, or evil aristocrats give way to common criminals, madmen, and scientists and later on, indicate the embodiment of tendencies that are repressed, or "'abjected' within a specific culture" (Punter and Byron 2004, 264). The exotic and distanced horrors found in earlier Gothic texts have now been replaced with something more disturbingly familiar and ambivalent. Works such as R. L. Stevenson's *Dr. Jekyll and Mr. Hyde* (1886), Oscar Wilde's *The Picture of Dorian Gray* (1891), H. G. Wells' *The Island of Dr. Moreau* (1896), and others "all draw their power from the fears and anxieties" that arise from the discourse of degeneration, and "the horror they explore is the horror prompted by the repeated spectacle of dissolution – the dissolution of the nation, of society, of the human subject itself" when freed from the constraints of social and ethical taboos essential for the stability of both society and the individual (Byron 2012, 187). This being said, there is the need to identify what is threatening, in the hope that it can be controlled, contained, and redefined, so that the boundaries this threatening other seems to destabilize are (re-)established (187). The specific nature of this threat as an external threat becomes more prominent during the late Victorian age and the twentieth century often being exemplified as a threat from other imperial powers or that "of the 'supposedly' civilized world being taken over by 'primitive forces'" (qtd. in Byron 2012, 187). As a matter of fact, similar concerns about the threat to the idea of nation and empire already characterized Gothic literature of the time but appeared to become more prominent with the decline of the British Empire as an imperial power in the post-war period.

Indeed, the years after the Second World War saw a gradual change in the landscape of British fantasy literature in both metaphorical and literal ways, with the early 1950s becoming a transitional moment regarding the representations of home, (national) identity, and empire. Again, within this context, the notion of the monster becomes slightly different with the other now signifying the outsider, the foreigner whose proximity is deemed threatening for the Western home-space. Through the spatial binary as indicated by the homely West and the dangerous East, Tolkien evidently provides another dichotomy, one that perpetuates the notion of the outsider and places it in binary opposition to those individuals that seemingly belong to the collective Western (national) identity (this includes humans, Elves, Hobbits, Dwarves). The conception of the West Country as an affective and collective (national) home-space therefore brings forward the question of inclusion and assimilation with regard to those deemed as outsiders. It becomes apparent that within the context of post-imperial melancholia, the desire "for a partial restoration [of England's] long-vanished homogeneity" becomes more prominent with Englishness now being profoundly racialized and notably threatened in view of postcolonial citizen-migrants arriving in the country (Gilroy 2004, 95). This fear of the "alien" or the (monstrous) stranger and the fantasy of them being too close to home or infiltrating the homogeneous nation-space therefore requires establishing new ways "of telling the difference, [and inventing] new forms of detection" or surveillance in an attempt to differentiate between the familiar and those who are not (Ahmed 2000, 2). By orientalizing the other, that is, the humanoid races that apparently serve as the Dark Lord's evil followers within the text, the alien "recuperates all that is beyond the human into the singularity of a given form" (2); the stranger is ultimately reduced to its stereotypical evil characteristics with its threatening/ monstrous nature residing in its proximity to the familiar home-space. This figure of the outsider, or stranger, positioned in the affective space and within the nation therefore becomes of paramount significance and indicates the primary figure of the post-war Gothic monstrosity.

In an attempt to define who can be assimilated in the core of the (English) nation-space since "nations become imagined and contested through the recognition of strangers", Sara Ahmed proposes a differentiation between those strangers whose appearance of difference can be claimed by the nation due to several partial similarities, and those who "may yet be expelled", as their prominent differences endanger the well-being of even the most heterogenous of nations (2000, 97). Within this context, it becomes apparent that only those who possess certain, pure, quintessential English characteristics, that is, the characters modeled after certain aspects of Englishness and inhabit the familiar key sites for home, can be integrated in the nation-space while the orientalized other becomes displaced and eventually excluded or even eliminated. In this sense, Tolkien's well-ordered Hobbits, "a little people, smaller than Dwarves [...] a merry folk [...] dressed in bright colors" with good-natured, bright faces, "hospitable and delighted in parties" (*FR*, 'Prologue', 2), Dwarves (tough craftsmen, though "not evil by nature" (*RK*, 'Appendix F', 1488) and noble, immortal Elves or "Fair Folk" function as the figure of the familiar stranger, in Ahmed's terms, namely, the stranger who though appears different to an extent (despite being humanoid, these races are not Men), is the same underneath (they are essentially white, and therefore benevolent). These familiar strangers can be assimilated, and even welcomed to the homely nation-space, as long as they enhance its illusion of appearing heterogeneous or multicultural. It is not a surprise that throughout the literary text, no one evidently questions their benevolence and integration in the Western collective (national) identity. Upon a closer look, the reader notices the extraordinary beauty of the Elves, with Faramir noting their reputation for being "wondrous fair to look upon" (*TT*, 'Of Herbs and Stewed Rabbit', 859) and Legolas being "fair of face beyond the measure of Men", singing elven songs in a clear, melodic voice "as he walked in the morning" (*RK*, 'The Last Debate', 1141). In addition, the beauty of both Galadriel and Arwen is widely praised by both the narrator and the characters, a fact that permeates the literary text and is notably encountered as Frodo lays his eyes on Arwen Undómiel for the very first time. What is being highlighted here is her "white arms and clear [...] flawless and smooth face [...] the light of stars [being] in her bright eyes", and her queenly appearance (*FR*, 'Many Meetings', 296).

Slender, graceful, and strong, the Elves become an inextricable part of the Western civilization in the secondary world, bearing certain similarities with the declining English aristocracy and nobility after the end of the 19th century. Illustrated as a race valiant, "high and beautiful" and fair of skin, these "older Children of the world" suggest a sense of purity, a timeless tradition that encompasses the legendarium and provides the basis upon which the narrative unfolds (*RK*, 'Appendix F', 1495). The proximity of the familiar strangers within the affective nation-space is evidently welcomed in this sense, supposedly creating a sense of multiculturalism, one that enables the nation to become "imagined and embodied as a space, not simply by being defined against other spaces, but by being defined as close to some others […] and further away from other others" (Ahmed 2000, 100). Under this scope, Aragorn's wedding to Arwen Undómiel in the City of Kings (*RK*, 'The Steward and the King', 1274) evokes the aforementioned notion; by serving as a way of (re-) establishing cultural difference within the nation-space, their union enables the latter to imagine itself as heterogeneous, grounded in tradition and profoundly inclusive. Interestingly, any restriction imposed by their supposed difference/definition of culture becomes abstracted and vague as she, who appears culturally different, can display her difference "only in such a way that it supplements what is already assumed to be the coherence of (the nation's) culture itself" (Ahmed 2000, 105), that is, the aspect of whiteness that they both have in common.

At this point, it is worth mentioning that through Tolkien's portrayal of Western characters as pure and benevolent defenders of the familiar and homely landscapes against the invasion of the other, the Orient is further fetishized and represented as "a chaotic, alien space, a place where the 'native' peoples are different from the Westland heroes, in need of […] destruction" (Balfe 2004, 79). With the nation signifying primarily a space of belonging and (national) identity being constantly re-shaped and (re-)imagined, produced only "through the differentiation between familiar and strange", the role of the stranger becomes essential and internal, in a sense, to the formation of the nation

(Ahmed 2000, 100). By determining whom the Western nation cannot include, Tolkien further defines (national) identity in terms of frontiers. It becomes apparent that, by being encountered at close proximity and experienced as threatening to "the coherence of national identity" (100) or its supposed multiculturalism, these monstrous strangers provide the necessary framework against which the benevolent nation becomes realized. The supposed barbarous nature, dreadful appearance and the threat that resides in the orientalized other arguably serve not only as a means to disrupt the boundaries of the previously mentioned affective home-spaces but as a means to construct the figure of the Gothic monster or the stranger stranger in the context of the post-war period. According to Ahmed, the appearance of these strangers reveals only "a strange being", one that cannot be assimilated and hence enables "the 'limit' of the multicultural nation to resurface" (2000, 106). This figure of the (monstrous) stranger within the literary text is notably encountered as the reader is introduced to the appearance of the Enemy, and the humanoid races that come to his aid. In this context, the Orcs, malicious and hateful creatures "first bred by the Dark Power of the North in the Elder Days" with their brutal language based on other tongues perverted to their own liking, "scarcely sufficient even for their own needs, unless it were for curses and abuse" (*RK*, 'Appendix F', 1486), wicked trolls and the cruel Men of Harad with their "[d]ark faces […] round shields, yellow and black with big spikes" from the hot South are portrayed as innately malevolent, degenerate races that can by no means identify themselves with the Western nation-space (*TT*, 'The Black Gate is Closed', 844). This idea becomes more prominent as the initial Quest becomes realized – as a matter of fact, the prevalence of the Captains of the West against Mordor's evil forces (re-)raises the question of the stranger in terms of what will befall those who inhabit Mordor and supported the Dark Lord in one way or another:

> The Captains bowed their heads; and when they looked up again, behold! Their enemies were flying and the power of Mordor was scattering like dust in the wind. As when death smites the swollen brooding thing that inhabits their crawling hill and holds them all in sway, ants will wander witless and purposeless and then feebly die, so the creatures of Sauron, Orc or troll or beast spell-enslaved, ran hither and thither mindless; and some slew themselves, or cast themselves in pits, or fled wailing back to hide in holes and dark lightless places far from hope. But the Men of Rhûn and of Harad, Easterling and Southron, saw the ruin of their war and the great majesty and glory of the Captains of the West. And those that were deepest and longest in evil servitude, hating the West, and yet were Men proud and bold, in their turn now gathered themselves for a last stand of desperate battle. But the most part fled eastward as they could; and some cast their weapons down and sued for mercy. (*RK*, 'The Field of Cormallen', 1242-3)

As the passage concludes, it becomes apparent that the literary text suggests a certain philosophy of purity: since they cannot escape the pre-defined identity they were assigned by the supposedly multicultural nation-space or even discard their initial evil purpose themselves after they are defeated, those displaced or condemned races are to be eliminated. As the notion of the Gothic monster and what it entails is projected onto this figure of the stranger it seems that the fears concerning the instability of identity that were apparent in the Gothic of the late Victorian period evinced by various representations of the metamorphic body that cannot be contained within any stable binaries, give way to the anxiety regarding the instability and ambivalence of national identity in a fast-moving multicultural world. The inability of those strangers to mask their orientalist appearance and innate wickedness makes it impossible for them to be assimilated and deems it necessary that they be eliminated. As Ahmed very eloquently points out, this sense of multiculturalism as an official discourse "involves narratives of partial assimilation or incorporation" through which the collective identity of the supposedly heterogeneous nation only appears different (2000, 106). The figure of the familiar stranger within Tolkien's work therefore allows the Western nation-space "to be(come) different and to have difference" as is underlined by the great variety of benevolent races that inhabit the secondary world. In contrast, the figure of the stranger or the monstrous other who is still recognized in its very "strangerness", entirely disappears, illuminating the aspects of alterity the nation cannot or will not include (107).

Through those literal monstrous bodies, the position of the stranger as the monstrous other and its treatment in *The Lord of The Rings*, it can be implied that Tolkien's literary multiculturalism appears vague and offers fruitful ground to be questioned. As Amy Kaplan points out, "domestic metaphors of national identity are intimately intertwined with renderings of the foreign and the alien, and […] the notions of the domestic and the foreign mutually constitute one another in an imperial context" (2002, 4). Under this scope, despite displaying a supposedly culturally inclusive approach towards the outsider, the text proposes at certain points an essentialist approach of inclusion, one that is grounded in racial features and functions as a frontier against which the nation itself becomes realized and imagined as innately benevolent. The Gothic monster, at this point, has been transformed to a great extent, in turn, coming to embody the fears and anxieties encountered in post-war Britain. As a matter of fact, the destructive "postimperial hungering" for renewed greatness that became prominent after the Second World War was embedded in the fantasy literature of the post-war period, proposing an idea of Englishness deeply racialized and equivalent to whiteness, one that draws from the nation's pastoral past, and builds upon a supposed multiculturalism within its borders (Gilroy 2004, 103). Within this context, the Gothic monster signifies the outsider, or the stranger stranger whose proximity is threatening to the homogeneity or supposed heterogeneity of the Western country.

Bibliography

Ahmed, Sara, *Strange Encounters: Embodied Others in Post-Coloniality*, (London: Routledge, 2000).

Balfe, Myles, 'Incredible Geographies? Orientalism and Genre Fantasy', *Social & Cultural Geography*, 5.1, (2004), 75-90 <10.1080/1464936042000181326>

Byron, Glennis, 'Gothic in the 1890s', in *A New Companion to the Gothic*, ed. by David Punter (Hoboken, NJ: Wiley-Blackwell, 2012), pp. 186-196.

Gilroy, Paul, *After Empire: Melancholia or Convivial Culture?*, (London: Routledge, 2004).

Kaplan, Amy, *The Anarchy of Empire in the Making of US Culture*, (Cambridge, MA: Harvard University Press, 2002).

McEvoy, Emma, 'Gothic Traditions', in *The Routledge Companion to Gothic*, ed. by Catherine Spooner and Emma McEvoy (London; New York: Routledge, 2007), pp. 7-10.

Punter, David, and Glennis Byron, *The Gothic*, (Malden, MA: Blackwell Publishing, 2004).

Tolkien, J.R.R., *The Fellowship of The Ring*, (London: Harper Collins Publishers, 2007).
—, *The Return of The King*, (London: Harper Collins Publishers, 2007).
—, *The Two Towers*, (London: Harper Collins Publishers, 2007).

Tolkien's Triptych: Ecological Uncanny, Double Dualism Personified, and the Language of the Literary Gothic

Michael Dunn

In William Wordsworth's poem *The Tables Turned* (1798) we are confronted with the even more infamous adage that has inherently become idiomatic: "we murder to dissect" (1911: 29, 481)[1] which is an important message for those of us studying literature and one that keeps our lofty elaborations and lamentations from being exceeded. However, one of the most fascinating and exhilarating things about Tolkien's work is that he invites us to dissect; and although he was an author who famously detested allegory and much preferred the subjective realm of so-called 'history' to over analysis, the inevitable use of allegory, both literary and linguistic, asks us to explore this literary labyrinth. The linguist eventually outweighs the writer or, better said, these two aspects of Tolkien's intrinsic essence are fully realised in the elaborate Arda that he created. We can appreciate the beauty of Tolkien's prose as we wander through a time "when first the shaggy woods unfurled" and "before the sun and moon we know / were lit to sail above the world" (*Lays*, 171; III: 402-3) all the way to the "monsters in the dark, and long, / long watches in the haunted night" while also enjoying the linguistic games that Tolkien constantly played (*Lays*,

---

1. Poetry references refer to page, verse, and line number respectively.

176; III: 588-9).[2] Not only is Middle-earth steeped in Gothic inspirations, with nature and the ecological world more akin to Dark Romanticism than its literary and artistic predecessor Romanticism, but the language Tolkien uses and creates is also equally steeped in the literary tradition that explores the darker recesses of the human imagination, liminality, and milieu-specific anxieties, and, additionally, the language of the genre and the Gothic language itself, as well as the cultures of the peoples that spoke it.

The Lord of the Rings marked a tipping point for unapologetic fantasy fiction whereby, according to Edward James, "[a]fter 1955 fantasy writers no longer had to explain away their worlds by framing them as dreams, or travellers' tales, or by providing them with any fictional link to our own world at all" (2012, 65). Although unapologetic as a unique wonder of worldbuilding and self-referential severity, Tolkien's work is riddled with aspects of both the literary Gothic tradition, landscapes, and language; so much so, in fact, that these inspirations themselves become distinctly uncanny as they creep up again, haunting the text with their eerie primarily extradiegetic but nonetheless intradiegetic presence.

1 - Ecological Uncanny and Environment

The Gothic aspects of Tolkien's texts are often presented as a triptych covering environments, peoples/monsters, and finally languages. It is apt then to start with the land as even fictional environments exist before peoples and creatures as well as constructed concepts such as language. Although both

---

2. *The Lays of Beleriand*, specifically *The Lay of Leithian*, originally published in 1985 and edited by Christopher Tolkien, is quoted here from the first of a three-volume deluxe edition of *The History of Middle-earth* (2017).

the 'construction' of language and the question of 'what came
first' are almost impossible to answer when it comes to Tolkien
as they are so inherently entwined and Tolkien unfortunately
passed away long before cognitive linguistics overtook Noam
Chomsky's generative grammar. Nevertheless, let us first and
foremost take a trip through this wondrous world of intricately
interconnected dichotomies where we not only find ourselves
in sublime and prelapsarian places of natural beauty such as
Lothlórien where "all the sky was blue" (*FR*, 'Lothlórien',
350) but also the dismal, dark depths of "Morgoth's dungeons
vast and drear" (*Lays*, 193; IV, 1151). Despite these depictions
of pastoral and dystopian places existing in stark antithesis
to one another in their sublime beauty and overwhelming
abjection "[a]ll that is Gold does not glitter" (*FR*, 'The Council
of Elrond', 247) as there also exists the uncanny eeriness
of Fangorn Forest, the Dead Marshes, the Barrow-downs,
Dunharrow, and the Dwimorberg; not only the singularity of
dread and despair seen in the fortress of Utumno or its Third
Age equivalent Barad-dûr.

Tolkien is not only intrigued by sublime beauty as seen in
the romance of ruins such as Amon Sûl – or indeed the mines of
Moria for that matter – but also, and possibly more importantly,
the in-between space of the ecological uncanny, which was
first seen in his own literary inspirations and reworking of the
Finnish myth the *Kalevala*. In his essay on the *Land of Heroes*,
which was an inspiration for his own *The Story of Kullervo*, he
says of the innately Gothic setting: "So much for religion, if
you can call it such, and the imaginary background. The real
scenery of the poems, the place of most of its action is Suomi
the Marshland: Finnland [sic] as we call it or as the Finns often
call it the Land of Ten Thousand Lakes" (*Kullervo*, 83). In a later
draft of the same essay, he goes on to directly state that "one

does sometimes hear the Kalevala, and things like it, cited as evidence of the enduring paganism of Europe that (we are told) is still fighting a gallant and holy battle against the oppression of Christianity, and of Hebraic Biblicality" (113). This so-called pagan and unbridled, often darker nature is equally foregrounded as more sublime and esoteric aspects of Tolkien's natural world. According to June-Ann Greeley, although an avid lover of nature, Tolkien "was not, however, sentimental or romantic about nature: rather, he was keenly aware of an energetic dynamism he sensed throughout and within the natural world" (2020, 125); as such, Tolkien opposed the 'control' and 'conquer' of nature and, instead, constantly imbues nature with its own sense of power. The Dead Marshes whose, according to one of Gollum's many meaningful songs, "rocks and stones / are like old bones" is a harsh and barren land, as well as perfectly pathless establishing it as a pagan landscape similar to that in Kullervo and, more generally speaking Finland (*TT*, 'The Passage of the Marshes', 620). Although life flourishes in the beautiful surroundings of Finland, the Dead Marshes, on the other hand, are first described as "The banks became moss-grown mounds. Over the last shelf of rotting stone the stream gurgled and fell down into a brown bog and was lost. Dry reeds hissed and rattled though they could feel no wind" (625). The anthropomorphism of nature is reflected in the grim and ghastly noises of hissing and gurgling. The landscape itself is haunted, and not only in its descriptions as grim and ghastly but also by the endless souls of soldiers trapped in a liminal space of undeath. Tolkien takes the reader on an anti-Proustian journey of terrible senses as Sam, Frodo, and Gollum are all about to enter this dreadful environment: "The reek of them [the pools] hung stifling in the still air" (625). The reader not only hears the terrible sounds of this Gothic landscape but can also smell it. A first-class lesson in sensory exploration becomes fully realized when Gollum, one of the only creatures – or creatures capable of narrative retelling – to have explored these roads untrodden since the Battle of Dagorlad, declares that he "used eyes and feet and nose" to navigate the uncanny landscape (625). Gollum's senses are conflated with the sensory power of the landscape itself; a lesson which many could learn from concerning our current entanglement with the environment as, according to Flore Coulouma, "death by nature is now a realistic prospect for much of the world's population," and despite being unable to see the extent of atmospheric carbon dioxide, the effects extend evermore outward accelerating our interdependency (2021, 59). Here we begin to see Gollum's exile, torture, and addiction[3] begin to blur at the lines between the displaced Gothic environment and the once Hobbit. Gollum the endless wanderer and last of his community, having experienced a Freudian psychosis of magnanimous proportions, is most at home in these haunted and ecologically uncanny places precisely because he too is haunted. This becomes most obvious when we hear, for the very first time, of Bilbo Baggins's homely Hobbit hole in direct juxtaposition with a "dirty, wet hole, filled with the ends of worms and an oozy smell" which we can assume perfectly surmises the sad and solitary confines of Gollum/Sméagol's sanctuary (*Hobbit*, 'An Unexpected Party', 11).

This concept of the haunted landscape takes on yet another interesting and nonetheless problematic aspect when we take

---

3. Vampiric thirst for blood being a very powerful metaphor for addiction in its many forms in a whole host of vampire literature classics as well as films. For two contemporary explorations see *Let the Right One In* [*Låt den rätte komma in*] (2009) for a juxtaposition between blood addiction and sexual perversion and also *Empire of the Vampire* (2021) for a link to substance abuse.

the 'real-world' filmic Middle-earth of Aotearoa/New Zealand as a physical monument to the crippling and corrosive powers of colonialism, 'contested' land, and the structural repressiveness of settler colonialism or, as Malcom Ferdinand in his brilliant new book *Decolonial Ecology* calls it, the "rupture of the relationship to the land" which encompasses other ruptures such as the rupture of biodiversity, plants, and animals (2022, 54). As Lewis Williams notes, "Indigenous scholars in both countries[4] point out, the terrain of Indigenous intergenerational connectivity is invariably permeated and fractured by colonial legacies as well as their ongoing structures" (2022, 52). New Zealand tourism, for example, exists primarily in accordance with the idea of untouched, utopian nature, with a lack of focus upon the disturbed nature of settler colonialism and the question of uncanny, unhomely, and unsustainable settler synergies.

How these fractures and disturbances affect characterisation is most obviously seen in Gollum/Sméagol. While the doppelganger of the later Victorian age was typified much earlier in James Hogg's *The Private Memoirs and Confessions of a Justified Sinner* (1824) and again at the end of the century in its more Gothic variation in Oscar Wilde's *The Picture of Dorian Gray* (1890) – both books that deal with morality informed by strict societal theology reflecting a genuine trope of the time: the myth of the Victorian gentleman and repression) – it is in *The Strange Case of Dr. Jekyll and Mr. Hyde* (1886) where the inspiration for Gollum/Sméagol's true Gothic double first finds form. Mr. Enfield, the Sherlock Holmesesque self-declared detective of the novella first explores the doubling of Hyde/Jekyll – as does Tolkien – through the landscape: "somebody must live there," asks Enfield rhetorically, "and

4. Both countries i.e. settler colonial New Zealand and Indigenous Aotearoa.

yet," he goes on, "it's not so sure; for the buildings are so packed together about that court, that it's hard to say where one ends and another begins" (Stevenson 2012, 6). Just as the fog bound and cramped streets of Victorian London were "linked to a tendency to degeneration" and, as such, represent the inner psychosis of Jekyll and his alter ego, Gollum's ecologically uncanny surroundings mimic his mania (Dryden 2003, 8). It becomes almost impossible for us as readers to see where the streets of London and the haunted landscape of Middle-earth, as well as both Jekyll and Sméagol's alter egos, begin and where they end. Through the blurring of boundaries, the novel, literally concocted in a feverish dream by Stevenson, explores the transgression of binaries of the potential for human good and evil as well as obsession and addiction; all of which are themes that follow Gollum/Sméagol all the way into the fires of Mount Doom which is not only an apocalypse for Middle-earth but also a personal apocalypse (meaning both revelation and annihilation) and end to their struggles.[5]

2 - Peoples and Monsters of Middle-earth

It is my suggestion that in Tolkien's work, where the dichotomy of good and evil is far more intricately entwined, not only is Gollum a true double, as is Dr. Jekyll and Mr. Hyde, which is nevertheless also a reflection of an internalized psychosis, but the work itself explores how evil ultimately stems from good; representing what Randel Helms called Tolkien's "puzzlement and fascination of evil" (1976, 37). Melkor was once one of the Ainur which, if we look past the more obvious analogy to Satan and the fall of the angels, tells us that, unlike Stevenson,

---

5. I.e. Gollum/Sméagol; the pronoun is intentional.

Tolkien was aware that without darkness there can be no light. The Great Music, the initial creation myth of Middle-earth, was woven from the time of its inception with discord by Melkor; thus evil existed in the very fabric of Tolkien's world from the time of its creation. Tolkien's universe, as such, was never a utopian, Hobbesian paradise. Many of Tolkien's characters, as well as creatures, exhibit aspects of both moral binaries; not merely unsightly and crippled creatures such as Gollum but also Galadriel whose mighty power would consume her if she gave in to the power of the Ring. Even Frodo, who always strives to do what is right, must learn essential lessons in morality from Gandalf when the wizard suggests "do not be too eager to deal out death in judgement" (*FR*, 'The Shadow of the Past', 59). In this regard, Tolkien's work is innately Gothic in that it exists to explore the uncomfortable possibility of horrendous deeds in all of us and the barrenness of many of Middle-earth's natural environments act as undead corpses that bear witness to tell of said tragedy and trauma. Andrew Smith and Williams Hughes, for example, explore how "the Gothic's representation of 'evil' can be used for radical or reactionary ends" and how ecoGothic, a term coined within their work, rejects or criticizes "ownership over nature" (2013, 2, 3). Once again, Tolkien's work can be read in distinct opposition to the Romantic in that it not only attempts to dissuade capitalist and technocratic consumption of nature via moral judgments of evil characters and creatures and their wrongdoings – i.e. Melkor, Sauron, or Saruman's rape of the earth – but also explores the true expanse of nature's great and terrifying turbulences represented in places such as the walls of Minas Morgul once "an eastern outpost of the defences of Ithilien" which is, at the time of *The Return of the King*, "held by evil things" (*RK*, 'The Tower of Cirith Ungol', 900); whose walls represent bestial fangs when Sam describes it as "jagged with crags like fangs that stood out black against the red light behind them" (899). According to Fred Botting this is precisely the purpose of Gothic: "the fabulously textual nature of narrative composition" and, as such, the creation of a "fabricated history, a fantasy of cultural and familial origins that belatedly – supplementarily – inscribes itself with morality and significance" (1999, 21). Nature, in Tolkien's cosmovision, along the lines of this fabricated history imbued with morality, thus refuses categorisation, aestheticization, romanticisation, and mechanisation; instead, it wields a wondrous power in a way that is supranatural as opposed to sublime.[6] However, this kind of ecological uncanny, or what Sladja Blazen amongst others have called 'haunted nature,' as opposed to Romantic dualism seen in Tolkien's natural world, is also found in his creatures and peoples.

Tolkien is seemingly obsessed with the ghosts of the past (both fictional and literal), as Christine Berthin suggests, *Frankenstein*, a text which so obviously inspired Tolkien's own synthetic creations of Orcs and Uruk-hai, can be read "symptomatically as a pathological refusal to let the dead die" (2010, 89). From the synthetic reanimation of dead Men and Elves, the zombified Nazgûl whose unnatural extended lifeforce is intrinsically and imminently linked to their overbearing overlord in a disturbing master/slave dynamic, Gollum's unnaturally extended long life and even the immortality of the Elves, and the Men of the mountains that literally haunt the tautological Dwimorberg as a dead people, super- or supra-naturally extended life run through all the tales of Middle-earth like veins through a body. The most obvious Gothic inspiration for the undead to have permeated Tolkien's

---

6. The Ents fully epitomise this supranatural anthropomorphism.

tropes is vampires. The only named vampire in Tolkien's books is Thuringwethil which is, as always, an elaborate wordplay using the author's invented languages. For example, *thurin* (meaning secret, hidden) combined with *gwath* (meaning shadow) creates a 'woman of secret shadow.' Thuringwethil is a bat-like creature most likely a combination of literary and mythological creatures similar to the winged *striges* of Greco-Roman antiquity but, in essence, she has the same traits as the prototypical vampire in literary tradition. Even in the Third Age of Tolkien's Arda, where this singular and obscure vampiric character plays no role, we still find traces of vampires. Orcs, according to Tolkien, "actually drink the blood of their victims," revealing that Quenyan adjectives for Orcs in the legendarium such as *serkilixa* (meaning blood thirsty) are often actually literal rather than metaphorical (*Nature*, 176). Tolkien's Orcs, literary inventions which seem so unique in their distinction to other literary monsters of the mind, are actually, then, a conglomeration of Shelley's *Frankenstein* (i.e. a synthetically created creature) combined with the vampiric tendencies of some of the most famous literary legends such as Geraldine in Coleridge's *Christabel*, Le Fanu's *Carmilla*, and later Stoker's *Dracula*. While Elves represent the promise of a preordained religiously implicated afterlife, Orcs, in antithesis, represent Julia Kristeva's "potency of pollution", defilement, and abjection (1982, 69). Whilst Gollum/Sméagol embody the Gothic double they also embody the Gothic vampire. For example, they are granted unnaturally long life due to the power of the Ring and they disdain the sun: "'Day is near,' he whispered, as if Day was something that might overhear him and spring on him" (*TT*, 'The Passage of the Marshes', 621). While Gandalf retells of their attempts to track Gollum they are represented in the text as a Gothic folktale. "The

Woodmen," suggests Gandalf, "said that there was some new terror abroad, a ghost that drank blood. It climbed trees to find nests; it crept into holes to find the young; it slipped through windows to find cradles" (*FR*, 'The Shadow of the Past', 58). Sightings, whispers, and hearsay of a new terror abroad act as a breakdown between text boundaries; reflecting folkloric suburban and superstitious tales; suggesting that although fantastic creatures and malignant monsters alike roam free in Tolkien's world, the sheer abundance doesn't stop the average character reacting with realism to real-world folktales and mythology giving authenticity to Tolkien's text as well as the broader Gothic triptych.

3 - Language

Treebeard naming Orcs (*serkilixa*) as bloodthirsty and as flint hearted (*sincahonda*) reflects the nonmetaphorical nature of Gothic creatures in Tolkien's universe as well as simultaneously revealing their capacity of embodying both the Gothic trope of Promethean, synthetic procreation as well as their vampiric tendencies in the same literary monster. Orcs are 'flint hearted' not only because that is where the emotional centre is located in the peoples and creatures of Middle-earth but because they are literally the walking dead, zombified, now lacking in the live organs – i.e. hearts – that would make them fully human; and blood thirsty as they are literally vampiric creatures who drink the blood of their unfortunate victims.[7] Although, having

---

7. This obviously presents the reader with some inconsistencies. As such, it is important to remember Tolkien changed his mind various times concerning the creation of Orcs, but nonetheless it is equally important to make sense of the transliteral meaning behind these actually bloodthirsty creatures who are also beholden to their long dead, reanimated hearts.

been reborn from humanoids they act as testament, once again, to the nonbinary possibility for all of Men – i.e. humans – and Elves to become 'evil' or, at least, forced via tyrannical powers to commit atrocious deeds. Tolkien's inability and refusal to let the dead die is also, broadly speaking, reflected in his invented languages he undertook during, in his own words, "occasional thefts of time" (*Secret Vice*, 26). Although many of his languages, especially Black Speech, are created under the guise of phonetic symbolism which suggests certain sounds are naturally clustered together and better represent the feel of a word, other aspects of his invented language act as a commune with the dead. Tolkien's so-called secret vice of creating languages is a direct answer to the uncanny void of dead languages; Gothic being one of them. He says of Gothic that he attempted to provide "points of interest for a learned society which I hope may yet arise" even though these points of interest are rather crude fragments (12). Tolkien attempted to invent a language based on the fragments of Gothic called Gautisk as early 1911-1912 (44) and his almost obsessive need to create fictional languages that serve to elevate these fragments to the forefront tells us that we too, and not only as readers, are haunted by the dead languages that built our current ones, haunted by ancestors with whom we would lack the words to speak and ancestors that Tolkien so longed to speak to in their own long extinguished tongues.

4 - Conclusion

The extreme ambiguities in Tolkien's work seen in the peoples, places, and languages of Middle-earth afford us as readers to establish an ontology of Gothic with which to traverse his ecologically uncanny landscapes and ultimate Gothic aim;

looking past gods and mighty beings of the cosmological realm, McBride suggests it is precisely "the existence of the half-dead and the undead [which] reveals the ambiguity surrounding the concept of death" (2020, 215). Why wouldn't the tradition of the Gothic inspire Tolkien? In the end Arda is, to Tolkien, the beginning of our own world and these ecologically uncanny aspects of nature still have a lot to tell; especially as we move past the slow decay of climate change and are confronted with climate mitigation in the face of apathetic policy making and damming IPCC reports. At a time when, "[f]or the first time in planetary history," according to Elmer Altvater, "humanity – acting through capitalist imperatives – is organising nearly all its productive and consumptive activities by tapping (and depleting) the planets energetic and mineral reserves"[8] (2016, 145) Tolkien's ecological uncanny as well as extensive ambiguity towards mortality, immortality, peoples, places, and even language of Middle-earth, which itself is a cosmology of myth for our own distant past, are all the more important today than they ever have been as our interconnected and toxic planetary situation accelerates and at many forefronts of climate change entanglements to both landscape and environment become ever more interdependent.

---

8. The concentrated efforts of extractivism seen in the industrial destruction undertaken by Saruman are an obvious comparison to make here.

Bibliography

Altvater, Elmar, 'The Capitalocene, or, Geoengineering against Capitalism's Planetary Boundaries', in *Anthropocene or Capitalocene? Nature, History, and the Crisis of Capitalism*, ed. by Jason Moore (Oakland: PM Press, 2016), pp. 138-153.

Berthin, Christine, *Gothic Hauntings: Melancholy Crypts and Textual Ghosts*, (Hampshire: Palgrave, 2010).

Blazen, Sladja, *Haunted Nature*, (London: Palgrave Macmillan, 2021).

Botting, Fred, 'The Gothic Production of the Unconscious', in *Spectral Readings: Towards a Gothic Geography*, ed. by Glennis Byron and David Punter (London: Macmillan Press, 1999), pp. 11-36.

Coulouma, Flore, 'Ecocide and the Anthropocene: Death and the Environment', in *The Routledge Companion to Death and Literature*, ed. by W. Michelle Wang, Daniel Jernigan, and Neil Murphy (Oxon: Routledge, 2021), pp. 159-170.

Dryden, Linda, *Modern Gothic and Literary Doubles: Stevenson, Wilde and Wells*, (London: Palgrave, 2003).

Ferdinand, Malcom, *Decolonial Ecology: Thinking from the Caribbean World*, (Cambridge: Polity, 2022).

Greeley, June-Ann, 'The Fearsome Enchantment of Tolkien's Woods', in *Madness in the Woods: Representations of the Ecological Uncanny*, ed. by Tina-Karen Pusse, Heike Schwarz, and Rebecca Downes (Berlin: Peter Lang, 2020), pp. 119-144.

Helms, Randel, *Tolkien's World*, (Herts: Panther Books, 1976).

James, Edward, 'Tolkien, Lewis and the Explosion of Genre Fantasy', in *The Cambridge Companion to Fantasy Literature*, ed. by Edward James & Farah Mendlesohn (Cambridge: Cambridge University Press, 2012), pp. 62-78.

Kristeva, Julia, *Powers of Horror: An Essay on Abjection*, (New York: Columbia University Press, 1982).

Kristoff, Jay, *Empire of the Vampire*, (London: HarperCollins, 2021).

Lindqvist, John Ajvide, *Let the Right One In*, (London: Quercus, 2009).

McBride, Ben, *Tolkien's Cosmology: Divine Beings and Middle-Earth*, (Ohio: Kent State University Press, 2020).

Tolkien, J. R. R. *The Hobbit*, (London: Guild Publishing, 1987).
— *The Fellowship of the Ring*, (London: HarperCollins, 2005).
— *The Two Towers*, (London: HarperCollins, 2005).
— *The Return of the King*, (London: HarperCollins, 2005).
— *The Story of Kullervo*, ed. by Verlyn Flieger (London: HarperCollins, 2015).
— *A Secret Vice*, ed. by Dimitra Fimi and Andrew Higgins (London: HarperCollins, 2016).
— 'The Lays of Beleriand', ed. by Christopher Tolkien (London: HarperCollins, 2017).
— *The Nature of Middle-earth: Late Writings on the Lands, Inhabitants, and Metaphysics of Middle-earth*, ed. by Carl F. Hostetter (London: HarperCollins, 2021).

Wordsworth, William, 'The Tables Turned', in *The Poetical Works of William Wordsworth*, ed. by Thomas Hutchinson (London: Henry Frowde/Oxford University Press, 1911), pp. 481-482.

Williams, Lewis, *Indigenous Intergenerational Resilience: Confronting Cultural and Ecological Crisis*, (London: Routledge, 2022).

Smith, Andrew & Hughes, William, 'Introduction: Defining the EcoGothic', in *Ecogothic*, ed. by Andrew Smith and William Hughes (Manchester: Manchester University Press, 2013), pp. 1-14.

Zanger, Jules, 'Metaphor into Metonymy: The Vampire Next Door', in *Blood Read: The Vampire as Metaphor in Contemporary Culture*, ed. by Joan Gordon and Veronica Hollinger (Pennsylvania: University of Pennsylvania Press, 1997), pp. 17-26.

The Gothic and Environmental Bioethics: The 'Creepy' Bodies of Middle-earth

Journee Cotton

[Ecocriticism studies] the literary and cultural relationships of humans to the nonhuman world—to animals, plants, minerals, climate, and ecosystems. Adopting a specifically gothic ecocritical lens illuminates the fear, anxiety, and dread that often pervade those relationships: it orients us, in short, to the more disturbing and unsettling aspects of our interactions with nonhuman ecologies. (Keetley and Sivils 2018, 1)

The environmental writing of J.R.R. Tolkien ranges from flowering pastoral descriptions, following the tangling paths created by the roots of trees, long passages centring on the localities crossed by the characters, the Elves spiritual seeming connection to nature, to the Hobbit's innate appreciation of the ground as demonstrated by living "in holes in the ground, […] and in such dwellings, they still felt most at home" (*FR*, 'Prologue', 25). The environmental aspects of Tolkien's work have enjoyed a developing academic conversation due to the legible connection between the characters in *The Lord of the Rings* and the environment, allowing a critical appreciation of the environment.[1] The fantastic setting of Middle-earth allows a creative reassessment of what it means to live in an environment and how to interact with it. Not only does Tolkien's work allow ecocritical conversations, it is deeply impacted by the Gothic.

There is an intersection between the Gothic and Environmental Bioethical readings of bodies in Tolkien's *The Lord of the Rings* (1954-1955). The Gothic's influence is linguistically and stylistically pervasive throughout the narrative. However perceived, it has been a relatively overlooked period in Tolkien studies and more recently the conversation connecting the Gothic to his works is growing, as Nick Groom has observed (2014, 296). The text presents corporeality coded with Gothic imagery through a variety of 'creepy' bodies including the 'monstrous', supernatural, cursed, decaying, and dead. Instances of the Gothic in the text may be read in the bodies of the Uruk-hai and the landscape. Environmental Bioethics seeks to integrate ecology, biology, human values, and medicine in social structures that simultaneously foster the value of all living beings and the environment. In *Medical Ethics: A Very Short Introduction* Tony Hope explains that Environmental Bioethics include dilemmas arising from the use of resources that may give immediate benefit to humans, rather than to the detriment of others such as animals and the environment (2018, 10-1).

---

1. See Chris Brawley, 'The Fading of the World: Tolkien's Ecology and Loss in "The Lord of the Rings"', *Journal of the Fantastic in the Arts*, 18.3 (2007), ed. by Brian Attebery, 292–307, http://www.jstor.org/stable/24351004, Matthew Dickerson, and Jonathan Evans, *Ents, Elves, and Eriador: The Environmental Vision of J.R.R. Tolkien*, (Lexington: University Press of Kentucky, 2006), Lucas P. Niiler, 'Green Reading: Tolkien, Leopold and the Land Ethic', *Journal of the Fantastic in the Arts*, ed. by Brian Attebery, 10.3, (1999), 276–285, http://www.jstor.org/stable/43308393, Niels Werber, 'Geo- and Biopolitics of Middle-Earth: A German Reading of Tolkien's "The Lord of the Rings"', *New Literary History*, 36.2, (2005), 227-246, https://www.jstor.org/stable/20057890.

Thus, I shall offer a brief introduction to better situate reading this text at the intersectional levels of Environmental Bioethics and the ecoGothic.

1 - ecoGothic, Environmental Bioethics, and Tolkien

The ecoGothic is an emerging field of scholarship that explores the Gothic through the theoretical framework of ecocriticism. The environment, nature, and landscape are deeply embedded in the Gothic. E. Parker and M. Poland note that when:

> one considers some of the 'giants' of the Gothic canon [...] it quickly becomes clear that 'Nature', in its various forms, is integral to the Gothic. Nature is essential to the Gothic both in terms of *where* things take place and *how* things take place. That is to say, the natural world is dominant both as setting and as character. (2019, 2)

The beings and landscape appear to be interlinked so fundamentally to each other that one cannot be understood without being informed by the other. Ecocriticism has the potential to connect nonhuman relationships and realities to the anxieties of the human. Thus, an ecoGothic perspective widens the consideration of literature to engage with the phobias produced in a context where the environmental and the corporeal coexist. In Tolkien some of these anxieties are manifestly observable between the relationship with 'evil' spaces and 'monstrous' creations, such as the production of the Uruk-hai and the linked destruction of Isengard, as discussed below. In 'Theorising the ecoGothic' Simon Estok frames the ecoGothic as an opportunity to engage in ecological anxieties and become realistic about environmental issues of the current day (2019, 34). Thus, the developing field of ecoGothic, in which nature is given even greater attention as not only setting but as a character and considers ecological aspects, further situates the connection to reading of this text from an Environmental Bioethical lens. Environmental Bioethics considers not only the bodies of beings and animals, but encompasses the body, so to speak, of the earth into the consideration to ensure a holistic approach is taken.

Gothic literature is often used as a medium for engaging morally in ethical dilemmas, e.g., bodies being constructed as monstrous due to fear and anxieties existing around Othered bodies, such as Tolkien's construction of 'corrupted' bodies.[2] As Bioethics and the Gothic have historically been used to examine ethical issues in literature, this usage also provides the intersection to read bodies from an Environmental Bioethical framework. There are numerous scholarly texts available about this intersection, especially regarding *Frankenstein* (Cambra-Badii, Guardiola, and Baños 2021, 2). However, this has not been considered in depth regarding the intersecting frameworks of the Gothic and Bioethics in reading bodies in *The Lord of the Rings*. Bioethics shares the interest of reading bodies fraught with ethical dilemmas, such as the bodies found in *The Lord of the Rings* that are presented as a spectacle of 'unnatural' or

2. Ser Jack Halberstam, *Skin Shows: Gothic Horror and the Technology of Monsters*, (Durham: Duke University Press, 1995), Sara Wasson, 'Useful Darkness: Intersections between Medical Humanities and Gothic Studies', *Gothic Studies*, 17, (2015), 1-12, https://researchgate.net/publication/276127881_Useful_Darkness_Intersections_between_Medical_Humanities_and_Gothic_Studies, Sara Wasson, *Transplantation Gothic: Tissue transfer in literature, film, and medicine* (Manchester: Manchester University Press, 2020). Christopher Vaccaro, ed., *The Body in Tolkien's Legendarium: Essays on Middle-Earth Corporeality*, (Jefferson: McFarland & Company, Incorporated Publishers, 2013). *ProQuest Ebook Central*, https://ebookcentral.proquest.com/lib/exeter/detail.action?docID=1386978.

'creepy' bodies. In 'Useful Darkness: Intersections between Medical Humanities and Gothic Studies' Sara Wasson notes that: "[m]edicine and the Gothic have long been entangled"; furthermore, the corporeal serves as the intersection for these two fields due to their interest in "suffering bodies and with trapped protagonists, [...] the vulnerability of victims tormented", the "rich material for fantasies of bodies and minds constrained", and provides "an interest in the way medical practice controls, classifies and torments the body in the service of healing" (2015, 1). Wasson's observation about the Gothic's interest is also legible in Tolkien's works. *The Lord of the Rings* is filled with tormented bodies (Nazgûl, Uruk-hai, Gollum) and medical (even if sometimes also magical) treatments that attempt to heal bodies, such as the use of *Athelas* used to treat Frodo's wound. Groom also contemplates the connections between *The Lord of the Rings* and the Gothic noting the use of Gothic tropes such as "split personalities, derangement, ghostly presences, forgetfulness, and hauntings: [...] the split selves of Gollum and of multi-named characters, the Ringwraiths (both kings of Men and Nazgûl)" (2014, 299). Not only does Tolkien share an interest in the corporeal with the Gothic, but also its relationship to the landscape, as discussed above. The intertwined nature of the Gothic, environment, the body, and medicine have thus paved the way for interdisciplinary conversations focusing on the Environmental Bioethical aspects of such texts.

2 - The Ring as the Creature and Sauron as Frankenstein

The following may be considered as a case study to demonstrate how reading Tolkien at an intersectional level can shed new light on Tolkien's texts and show his work's ongoing relevance to our present anxieties. The instance of the experimental production of the One Ring may be seen as legible from both the Gothic and Environmental Bioethical stances. For instance, the comparison between Sauron as Frankenstein experimenting secretly in his 'laboratory', located in a volcanic mountain, later surrounded by an ashen (rather than arctic) wasteland, to produce something that many in Middle-earth believe should not be done, their Luciferian trajectory, and the resulting production of a monster. The Ring can be read as a biomedical technology; its occurrence provides fodder for conversations on the ethics regarding biotic and technological intervention without consent in other's bodies. For example, the Ring affects the bodies of any it encounters, it intervenes in ageing and causes instability in the corporeality of those beings. Another layer may consider the Ring as Frankenstein in its own way experimenting and intervening on the bodies it encounters in monstrous ways. In *Dangerous Bodies: Historicising the Gothic Corporeal* Marie Mulvey-Roberts notes:

> [a]s a body of writing, the Gothic has its own inherent dangers. Not only does it unlock taboos and collapse boundaries, but it can also generate and perpetuate negative stereotypes by stigmatising the inassimilable Other as dangerous body. The dread of difference is articulated through such bodies, particularly when seen as carriers of dangerous desires, incubators for destabilising ideas or containers of counter-hegemonic ideologies, normally related to race, class, religion, gender or sexuality [...] in arguing that the Other is illusory and deriving its power (or lack of it) from the subject, claims that this very illusion actually structures our (social) reality itself. (2016, 1)

These problematic elements in the reading of Gothic bodies are also found in Tolkien's works. Tolkien fixates on the idea of 'corruption' throughout his legendarium, especially regarding the bodies of many 'evil' creatures. This has some problematic elements which are beyond the scope of this current paper.[3] Therefore, this paper focuses on the ways society constructs 'creepiness' and its motivations for framing them as 'creepy' bodies. Thus, a significant caveat must be made in the reading of these 'creepy' bodies. From a bioethical perspective the 'creepiness' addressed shall refer to the societally problematic views of bodies that can cause differently abled bodies and those outside what is deemed by society as 'normative' to be cast as monstrous or 'Other' as a construct of the Gothic. So, perhaps the truly 'creepy' thing going on is the motivation, often driven by power or fear, to subjugate difference. Thus, readers may see glimpses in Tolkien's works of instances that promote bioethical values, or often moments that are problematic, as well as scenes that are somewhat ethical, but fraught with some issues, as is additionally often found in the Gothic.

3 - Biotic Tinkering to Create 'Designer Babies'

An example to consider concerns experimentation on bodies. Saruman's tinkering with the bodies of Men and Orcs appears to be akin to 'genetic' engineering. Much like the classic figure of *Frankenstein* 'creating' life by tinkering with the biotic, Saruman's production of the Uruk-hai may be read as 'creating new life' by means of genetically engineering 'designer babies'. In 'Geo- and Biopolitics of Middle-Earth: A German Reading of Tolkien's "The Lord of the Rings"' Niels Werber describes Saruman as "chang[ing] from a sorcerer into a genetic engineer,

---

3. I am, however, currently researching and addressing these concerns in my PhD thesis that considers Tolkien from a Environmental Bioethical perspective.

breeding his own new, strong, martial, cannibalistic Orc race of 'fighting Uruk-hai'" (2015, 230-1). Werber goes on to connect genetic engineering to genealogical issues of breeding and biopolitics. Werber continues by commenting that:

> [t]he descent of the Orc is unnatural and artificial. They were manufactured. The species came into being by genetic experiments, crossbreeding, and dark magic. [...] Orcs are the outcome of engineered processes of depravation [...] What they lack in comparison to their genetic ancestors is humanity and individuality (from the narrator's perspective) or weakness, hesitation, and disloyalty (from the perspective of the Dark Lord). Their depravation is, from another standpoint, their improvement in strength and obedience. (235)

This paper centres the conversation around the issue of eugenics brought up by genetic engineering. Genetic engineering, creating, or 'tampering' with the fundamental aspects of life is a question that intersects in the realms of the Gothic and Bioethics. Saruman appears to conduct 'gene therapy' to significantly alter an Orc and Man crossbreed to create Uruk-hai (*TT*, 'Treebeard', 90; 'Helms Deep', 167).

In 'Gene Editing: New Technology, Old Moral Questions' Brendan P. Foht recalls the problematic aspects of the early 20th century eugenics movement, that upheld "a set of ideas and policies notoriously aimed at perfecting the human race (or arresting its decline) by controlling human heredity" (2016, 9). He outlines the ideological issues pertaining to alterations done to the germline in accordance to the 'Eugenics Catechism' that sought to "preserve this precious protoplasm from the deterioration it faced" resulting in the problematic legacy in the United States of a "the practice of compulsory sterilisation of the so-called 'feeble-minded' and others judged genetically unfit. Such eugenic sterilisation was a perversion of the aims of medicine — surgically manipulating the bodies of patients not to preserve or restore their health but" for society-based desires (9). Although the text's stance on the issue is clear, condemning Saruman's genetic alterations and opening a conversation regarding the ethics of altering genetics and the creation of 'designer' babies, there is a need to acknowledge the problematic elements of the perspective; these beings, the Uruk-hai, appear to be read with some potentially eugenicist lens as their genetic makeup seems to equate their inability for 'goodness'. However, Saruman's motivation for tinkering shall remain the focus and be examined from a bioethical lens.

Saruman's treatment of vulnerable bodies seems hauntingly similar to bioethicist Foht's warning that genetic modification and intervention could result in parental "expectations [becoming] inscribed in" a child's "body" (15). Foht continues to describe the potential risk as a child's agency may:

> not only be disappointing his parents' expectations but also, in a sense, frustrating the design of his own nature, which has been deliberately shaped by his parents [...] the fact that parents have been susceptible to imposing their expectations of how their children should be is just what should make us suspicious of projects for human enhancement in the future [...] The legacy of the eugenics movement should teach us of the dangers of elevating abstractions like the 'germline' above the needs and medical interests of actual patients. [...] we must recognise the dangers of increasing our power over future generations. (15)

Returning to the threads of the Gothic and Bioethics, I suggest considering that their intersection allows an investigation of the impetus of the treatment of these 'Othered' bodies. So, in turn, for a Uruk-hai to do any less than Saruman's wishes would frustrate its very genetically embedded nature. Thus, this element of the Gothic highlights the line of questioning in Bioethics as Mulvey-Roberts observation:

> [t]he making of the Gothic world, as for any repressive institution of state, depends upon the consensual formation of a monstrous alterity, whether it be vampire, ghost, demonic stigmatic or man-made monster. The existence of otherness in the world is most apparent through its corporeality. Monstrosity is invariably a perception relating to inanity manifests as an object of fear. (2016, 3)

Saruman's motivation appears to be fear and delusion. He despaired that Sauron can be defeated, was seduced by flattery to believe himself able to overcome Sauron, and his actions are dictated by a grasp for power and self-preservation (*TT*, 'The Road to Isengard', 189). Saruman instrumentalises beings as weapons. He appears to be enacting policies of biopower and necropolitics through his intervention in the genetic makeup of beings to better instrumentalise them for his war and power over their, and other's, life and death. His fear causes him to dehumanise bodies of Orcs and Men and throughout the process of production he harms the surrounding landscape of Isengard and Fangorn Forest. Saruman seems to demonstrate what Keetley and Sivils observe in:

> human actions that bear upon nature (and how many of them do not?), continually fray into unforeseen consequences. At

the broadest level, then, the ecogothic inevitably intersects
with ecophobia, not only because ecophobic representations
of nature will be infused, like the gothic, with fear and dread
but also because ecophobia is born out of the failure of
humans to control their lives and their world. And control, or
lack thereof, is central to the gothic. (2018, 3)

This fear wreaks biotic havoc, its desolation is not isolated to
just the body of the peoples of Middle-earth, but additionally
the environment itself. Therefore, Saruman's un-bioethical
actions against the biotic is consistently implemented across
bodies in beings and 'nature'. In the end even nature revolts
against him.

4 - Conclusion

This paper seeks to demonstrate the intersection observable in
The Lord of the Rings through the elements of experimentation
and the production of 'creepy' or 'othered' bodies as a starting
point for an intersectional dialogue regarding the ethics
surrounding bodies and their treatment. Furthermore, as
discussed throughout, bodies and the environment, especially
read in the Gothic lens, are deeply interlinked. The desire
for control over bodies and the environment is demonstrated
throughout the biopolitical decision-making of characters
such as Saruman over the bodies of the Uruk-hai. Therefore,
I suggest considering this intersection allows a heightened
awareness to the narrative's contemplation of ethical issues as
well as providing a lens to consider how the Gothic elements
of this text are used to express ideological perspectives on
corporeality and their value.

Bibliography

Brawley, Chris, 'The Fading of the World: Tolkien's Ecology and Loss in "The Lord of the Rings"', *Journal of the Fantastic in the Arts*, 18.3 (2007), ed. by Brian Attebery, pp. 292–307, http://www.jstor.org/stable/24351004 [Accessed 20 October 2021]

Cambra-Badii, I., Guardiola, E., and Baños, J. E., 'Frankenstein; or, the modern Prometheus: a classic novel to stimulate the analysis of complex contemporary issues in biomedical sciences', *BMC Medical Ethics*, 22.17 (2021), 1-8, https://doi.org/10.1186/s12910-021-00586-7 [Accessed 14 June 2022]

Dickerson, Matthew, and Jonathan Evans, *Ents, Elves, and Eriador: The Environmental Vision of J.R.R. Tolkien*, (Lexington: University Press of Kentucky, 2006).

Estok, Simon C., 'Theorising the EcoGothic', *Gothic Nature*, 1, (2019), 34-53, https://gothicnaturejournal.com/wp-content/uploads/2019/09/Estok_34-53_Gothic-Nature-1_2019.pdf [Accessed 20 June 2022]

Foht, Brendan P., 'Gene Editing: New Technology, Old Moral Questions', *The New Atlantis*, 48, (2016), 3-15, *JSTOR*, http://www.jstor.org/stable/43766980 [Accessed 28 June 2022]

Groom, Nick, 'The English Literary Tradition: Shakespeare to the Gothic', In *A Companion to J.R.R. Tolkien*, ed. by Stuart D. Lee, (2014), pp. 286-302, https://doi.org/10.1002/9781118517468.ch20 [Accessed 15 May 2023]
—, *Twenty-First-Century Tolkien: What Middle-Earth Means To Us Today*, (London: Atlantic Books, 2022).

Halberstam, Jack, *Skin Shows: Gothic Horror and the Technology of Monsters*, (Durham: Duke University Press, 1995).

Hope, Tony, *Medical Ethics: A Very Short Introduction*, eds. Michael Dunn and Tony Hope, 2nd edn., (Oxford: Oxford University Press, 2018)

Keetley, D., and M. W. Sivils, 'Introduction: Approaches to the Ecogothic', in *Ecogothic in Nineteenth-Century American Literature*, ed. by D. Keetley and M. W. Sivils, (New York, New York, Routledge, 2018), pp. 1-20.

Mulvey-Roberts, Marie, *Dangerous Bodies: Historicising the Gothic Corporeal*, (Manchester: Manchester University Press, 2016), pp. 1–13, JSTOR, http://www.jstor.org/stable/j.ctt18pkdzg.5 [Accessed 14 Jun. 2022]

Niiler, Lucas P., 'Green Reading: Tolkien, Leopold and the Land Ethic', *Journal of the Fantastic in the Arts*, ed. by Brian Attebery, 10.3, (1999), 276–285, http://www.jstor.org/stable/43308393 [Accessed 05 October 2021]

Parker, E. and M. Poland, 'Gothic Nature: An Introduction', *Gothic Nature*, 1, (2019), 1-19, https://gothicnaturejournal.com/wp-content/uploads/2019/09/Parker-Poland_1-20_Gothic-Nature-1_2019.pdf [Accessed 05 May 2022]

Smith, Andrew, and Hughes, William, 'Introduction: Defining the EcoGothic', *EcoGothic*, eds. Andrew Smith and William Hughes, (2013), pp. 1–14, http://www.jstor.org/stable/j.ctt18mvk5r.5 [Accessed 29 June 2022]

Tolkien, J. R. R., *The Fellowship of the Ring*, (New York: The Ballantine Publishing Group, 1994).
—, *The Two Towers*, (New York: The Ballantine Publishing Group, 1994).

Vaccaro, Christopher, ed., *The Body in Tolkien's Legendarium: Essays on Middle-Earth Corporeality*, (Jefferson: McFarland & Company, Incorporated Publishers, 2013). *ProQuest Ebook Central*, https://ebookcentral.proquest.com/lib/exeter/detail.action?docID=1386978 [Accessed 30 November 2021]

Wasson, Sara, *Transplantation Gothic: Tissue transfer in literature, film, and medicine*, (Manchester: Manchester University Press, 2020)
—, 'Useful Darkness: Intersections between Medical Humanities and Gothic Studies', *Gothic Studies*, 17, (2015), 1-12, https://www.researchgate.net/publication/276127881_Useful_Darkness_Intersections_between_Medical_Humanities_and_Gothic_Studies [Accessed 18 June 2022]

Werber, Niels, 'Geo- and Biopolitics of Middle-Earth: A German Reading of Tolkien's "The Lord of the Rings"', *New Literary History*, 36.2, (2005), 227-246, https://www.jstor.org/stable/20057890 [Accessed 24 June 2022]

"The forest is *queer*" - The Fantastic and the Gothic in *The Lord of the Rings*

D.A.K. Watson

Tzvetan Todorov's *The Fantastic* (1975) presents an interesting dilemma for the student of fantasy literature. On the one hand, the title connects it etymologically with fantasy, something that seems fitting for a genre so influenced by J.R.R. Tolkien, and if one were to skim through the book for the works under discussion, the historical connection to fantasy literature through Gothic literature, ghost stories, and horror becomes apparent. On the other hand, as Brian Attebery notes in his essay on 'Structuralism' (2012), Todorov's Fantastic is not the same genre as fantasy, but instead a type of "eerie fiction" (88). Applying Todorov's concept of the Fantastic as a *genre* to a work such as *The Lord of the Rings* would thus create some very strange results, excluding Tolkien's work and indeed much that is foundation to the fantasy genre. This exclusion comes from Todorov's very narrow definition of the Fantastic as a hesitation between two other genres, the uncanny and the marvelous. The uncanny might be defined as "the supernatural explained" and the marvelous as "the supernatural accepted" (Todorov 1975, 41-2); thus, the uncanny includes any work where there is a natural or scientific explanation for a strange phenomenon, and the marvelous includes any work where the strange phenomenon is accepted without explanation. The

Fantastic, then, exists where the characters, the reader, or both are uncertain about the strange phenomenon, i.e., where there is a hesitation between the uncanny and the marvelous.

As might be apparent from this definition, maintaining this hesitation is difficult; very few works actually maintain this hesitation all the way through. Todorov himself acknowledges this difficulty and suggests that "If we do decide to proceed by examining certain parts of the work in isolation, we discover that by temporarily omitting the end of the narrative we are able to include a much larger number of texts within the genre of the fantastic" (43). While *The Lord of the Rings* clearly does not belong to the Fantastic, we can see that Tolkien makes use of the Fantastic as a mode throughout his work to build suspense in the reader, and this use is not an invention of Tolkien's but something that he inherited from the works that came before him, specifically the Gothic literature of the eighteenth and nineteenth centuries.

So, how do we recognize this hesitation between the uncanny and the marvelous that defines the Fantastic in *The Lord of the Rings*? Todorov explains that "Ambiguity results from the use of two stylistic devices which suffuse the entire text: imperfect tense and modalization" (38). While the imperfect tense is, as the translator of *The Fantastic*, Robert Howard, notes, "less apparent" (note on 38) in English, modalization – constructions that bring into doubt statements of fact – is noticeable in the model text Todorov uses, Nerval's *Aurelia*, with constructions that indicate uncertainty: "It seemed to me", "seemed to have known", "I believed", "I had the sense" and so on (qtd. in Todorov 1975, 38). When we see these particular constructions in great numbers, and when combined with the use of the supernatural, the author is using the Fantastic to express hesitation in the characters and cause suspense for the reader through that hesitation.

In *The Lord of the Rings*, the Old Forest sequence provides a prime example of this hesitation in action, which is not coincidentally the Hobbits' first adventure outside the bounds of the Shire and into the unknown. Tolkien sets our expectations of the Old Forest through Merry's description of it:

> But the forest is queer. Everything is very much more alive, more aware of what is going on, so to speak, than things are in the Shire [...] But at night things can be most alarming, or so I am told. I have only once or twice been in here after dark, and then only near the hedge. I thought all of the trees were whispering to each other, passing news and plots along in an unintelligible language; and the branches swayed and groped without any wind. They do say the trees do actually move (*FR*, 'The Old Forest', 110; emphasis original)

We can see Merry's uncertainty about the Old Forest in phrases like "so to speak," "so I am told," "I thought," and "They do say" so that even as he is reporting on things he has some direct knowledge of, Merry expresses doubt about his own interpretation of them. He continues this same hedging when discussing the paths that "seem to shift and change" (110).

This hesitation continues when the Hobbits enter the Old Forest. Where before we had Merry expressing uncertainty, now the narrator does so:

> as they went forward it *seemed* that the trees became taller, darker, and thicker [...] they all got an uncomfortable feeling that they were being watched with disapproval [...] The *feeling* steadily grew, until they found themselves looking

up quickly, or glancing back over their shoulders, *as if* they expected a sudden blow. (111)[1]

We might question why the narrator expresses the scene this way. For example, it is not unrealistic for the trees to become "taller, darker, and thicker" as one walks further into a forest; this would be quite natural. However, if we consider the passage without the hesitating language, we can see how the effect on the reader might change:

> as they went forward [...] the trees became taller, darker, and thicker [...] they were being watched with disapproval. The [disapproval] steadily grew, until they found themselves looking up quickly, or glancing over their shoulders, [...] [expecting] a sudden blow. (111)

While this passage can build some suspense through the increasing danger, the certainty of it lessens the effect, which is created not just from the danger but through the uncertainty of that danger. And this uncertainty continues throughout the Hobbits' journey, as "the air *seemed* heavy [...] The trees *seemed* to close in before them" (112) and "The path *seemed* to be making directly for [the river]" (113).

When the Hobbits directly encounter Old Man Willow, Tolkien varies between certainty and uncertainty in the narration. Frodo hears "a soft fluttering *as of* a song half whispered" that "*seemed* to stir in the boughs above," but then Frodo "saw leaning over him a huge willow-tree, old and hoary" (116); there may be uncertainty about the song, but not about the willow leaning over him. Merry and Pippin

---

1. Throughout the paper emphasis is mine except where stated.

experience something very similar as "it *seemed* that they could *almost* hear words" while the "great cracks gaped wide to receive them" (116). Thus, the narration expresses certainty about some things – there is no doubt about Merry and Pippin being almost devoured by a tree – while maintaining doubt about others, such as the singing.

For the characters, the spell is broken when Frodo is pushed into the river, fully wakes up, and runs for help, although he has no reason to think help will come. It does come, however, with the arrival of Tom Bombadil, who saves Merry and Pippin from Old Man Willow, and as Merry and Pippin emerge from the tree, and as the reader emerges entirely from the Fantastic, the hesitation in the narrator's language lessens. Instead, the reader is in what Todorov calls the "exotic marvelous" (1975, 55), where the characters and the reader are more willing to accept that this is just the way things are in this world. While neither we nor the hobbits ever get a full explanation of either Old Man Willow or Tom Bombadil, Treebeard does help to clarify Old Man Willow, explaining to Merry and Pippin that sometimes "you find that some [trees] have bad hearts" and that he "does not doubt there is some shadow of the Great Darkness lying there still away north; and bad memories are handed down" (*TT*, 'Treebeard', 468). With this we come to understand that trees like Old Man Willow are a part of Middle-earth, and so the reader fully emerges from the Fantastic into the marvelous. Tom Bombadil remains unexplained in the text, a truly marvelous figure that the characters accept as part of their world.

We see a similar pattern, where the characters have a fantastic encounter that emerges into the marvelous, in other parts of *The Lord of the Rings*. For example, when Merry and Pippin escape from the Uruk-hai and into Fangorn Forest, the scene begins similarly to that of the Old Forest, as "a queer stifling feeling came over them," but then Tolkien contradicts this through the narrator's clarification "*as if* the air were too thin or too scanty for breathing" (461). The uncertainty here is not only in what Merry and Pippin are experiencing but even in the narrator's description, as "stifling" and "too thin" are not usually synonymous. Both Pippin and Merry, however, immediately notice a difference between Fangorn and the Old Forest. Pippin compares Fangorn to the Old Took's room in the Great Place at Tuckborough, where "he [the Old Took] and the room got older and shabbier together," noting "but that's nothing to the old feeling of this wood" (461). Pippin's reference to the Old Took shows that there is not the same negative feeling here as there was in the Old Forest; Pippin's comparison is of Fangorn to something familiar and connected to home, as opposed to the uncanniness of the Old Forest. And as in the Old Forest before, when Merry and Pippin meet Treebeard, the master of Fangorn Forest, the uncertain language in the narration diminishes, and we are once again fully in the marvelous world.

Another example, although somewhat less definitive in terms of explanation, is the attempt by the Fellowship to cross the Redhorn Gate through the Misty Mountains. Here again we have much of that uncertain language, when they hear "eerie noises" that "*may have only* been a trick of the wind in the cracks and gullies of the rocky wall, but the sounds were those of shrill cries, and wild howls of laughter" (*FR*, 'The Ring Goes South', 289). Exactly what is responsible for the storm (apparently localized to just the Fellowship) remains somewhat uncertain; Gimli argues for Caradhras, the other name of the Redhorn, as an actual personage, the cruel spirit of the mountain. Boromir does suggest that Sauron could be behind it as well. Gimli expresses doubt about this, saying "His arm has grown long indeed," but Gandalf's reply ("His arm has grown long") still leaves open that possibility (288). Aragorn's explanation that "there are many evil and unfriendly things in the world" that "are not in league with Sauron" (289) agrees with Gimli's assessment, and when the Fellowship finally turns around and escapes, it is this explanation we are left with: "the malice of the mountain *seemed* to be expended, *as if* Caradhras was satisfied that the invaders had been beaten off and would not dare to return" (293). But here the narrator is not willing to fully agree with Gimli; the language of uncertainty remains, and even in the marvelous world of Middle-earth some things remain unexplained.

While these examples demonstrate the use of the Fantastic in *The Lord of the Rings* and help to show its effects on the reader, a question remains: is this a fundamental part of fantasy as a genre or are they a stylistic quirk of its author? Can we trace this in Tolkien's antecedents and see the relationship with the genres that preceded modern fantasy? A small sampling of authors whose works we know Tolkien was familiar with does show a similar use of the Fantastic to build the feeling of suspense in the reader. For example, in William Morris's *The Wood Beyond the World* (1894) – which we know Tolkien had in his library[2] – uncertainty and hesitation are continuously present until the last chapters of the book. Here, Walter, the son of a merchant and unhappily married to the daughter of a rival family, has a vision of three figures (a Lady, a Maid, and a Dwarf) for which he has no explanation. Each time he encounters them, they mysteriously disappear, but Walter finds himself compelled to seek after them, and after a series of misadventures, he finds himself in the titular Wood.

---

2. See Oronzo Cilli's *Tolkien's Library: An Annotated Checklist* (2019), "Morris, William"

Unlike the examples we have examined in *The Lord of the Rings*, the uncertainty relates not to the Wood itself, which is described as a pleasant and well-ordered place, but to the inhabitants, especially the Lady and the Maid. Clarence Wolfshohl observes that "Morris's young maiden becomes symbolic of that world, adding to its allure with her pseudo-supernatural powers" that "often tend to be suspect of dark deeds in […] Walter's (the hero's) mind […] and that is where the tension originates," noting that because "The reader recognizes the maiden's powers only through Walter's eyes […] the reader must feel as uneasy about the maiden as Walter often does" (1979, 29). While Walter essentially falls in love with the Maid at first sight, he continuously doubts her; he has only her word for much of what he understands about the situation, such as her assertions that the Lady, to whom she is bound as a slave, is an evil seductress. Walter does come eventually to trust her and the two end up as king and queen of a foreign land, but by this time the book is no longer interested in building tension but is instead seeking to resolve the story with a happy ending; the Maid, now queen and bereft of her magic after marriage, is exactly who she said she was.

Similarly to Morris's *The Wood Beyond the World*, George MacDonald's *Lilith* (1895) uses the Fantastic as an inciting incident that compels the protagonist forward. *Lilith* begins with the protagonist, Mr. Vane, having just recently returned to his family's estate to assume its management, reading in the library when he sees something for which he has no explanation:

> something, *I cannot tell what, made me* turn and cast a glance to the farther end of the room, *which I saw, or seemed* to see, a tall figure reaching up a hand to the bookshelf. The next instant, my vision *apparently* rectified by the comparative dusk, I saw no

one, and *concluded* that my optic nerves had been momentarily affected from within. (MacDonald 2000, 6-7)

Eventually his visions of the man result in him finding a mirror that proves to be a gateway to another world, where he encounters the man as a talking raven (Mr. Raven, in fact) and the beautiful and treacherous Lilith, who proves a vampiric seductress. Fairly soon into the book, however, Mr. Vane accepts the supernatural place and the events that occur there, and so the book moves fully into the marvelous after using the Fantastic as a springboard.

At this point we can see a distinct difference between the uncertainty and hesitation contained in Tolkien and that in Morris and MacDonald; where Tolkien focuses closely on the landscapes, in Morris and MacDonald it is focused more on the uncertainty of people, their intentions and even existence. Thus, we return to the question of inspiration, and it is here that Tom Shippey's consideration of *The Wood beyond the World* gives us insight into the problem. Of it he wrote:

> probably *The Wood beyond the World* was an element in the making of Lothlórien, or better still Fangorn, where also characters wander in a network of lies and glimpses and coincidences [...] However Tolkien could read sagas and romances as well as Morris [...] so that when one sees similarity it may not be descent from one to another, but rather descent of both from some centuries-old common source. (qtd. in Scull & Hammond 2006, 601)

Without a direct quote from Tolkien, or several very close examples from possible texts, even though we know that Tolkien was familiar with both works, the differences in their uses of the Fantastic are such that it is more likely that it comes from a common source. We do not have to look back centuries, however, to find that source, but only to the previous two centuries before *The Lord of the Rings*, and for that it is helpful to return to Todorov.

Todorov begins his discussion of the uncanny and the marvelous with the Gothic novel, where he observes what we have seen in the works of Tolkien, Morris, and MacDonald: "Here we find not the fantastic in the strict sense, only genres adjacent to it. More precisely, the effect of the fantastic is certainly produced, but during only a portion of our reading" (1975, 42). This connection to the Gothic novel as a precursor of the genre of the Fantastic also helps explain the presence of the Fantastic at times in works of modern fantasy; they are drawing from a common source of inspiration, from which they diverged in the mid-nineteenth century. As Anna Vaninskaya argues "the 'marvellous' or 'supernatural,' originally found in solution with a number of other elements, gave rise to several distinct lines of influence," including horror and science fiction, "while Morris, [H. Rider] Haggard, and MacDonald would be joined as the originators of modern fantasy, the ancestors of C.S. Lewis and J.R.R. Tolkien" (2008, 74). Vaninskaya further notes that while both MacDonald's *Lilith* and Haggard's *She* (1887) – another novel influential on Tolkien[3] – feature beautiful and immortal antagonists, "individually they may bear more formal affinity to a Gothic romance of Bram Stoker's than to each other," and that because of the differences of influence between Stoker on one hand and MacDonald and Haggard on the other, "both are firmly conjoined as progenitors of fantasy, while Dracula stands apart as a seminal text in the tradition of horror literature" (Vaninskaya 2008, 75).

---

3. See John Garth, *The Worlds of J.R.R. Tolkien* (2020), 38-9.

Thus, this descent of modern fantasy back through the late-Victorian romance to the Gothic novel helps us better understand Tolkien's use of the Fantastic in *The Lord of the Rings* and elsewhere. As Katarzyna Ferdynus observes, Gothic literature and modern fantasy draw largely from the same sources, including "the supernatural elements in legends and ballads, pagan Nordic and Celtic mythology, exoticism in oriental and eastern tales, and chivalric romances" (2016, 33). Ferdynus also explains that in the Gothic convention "the atmosphere of mystery and terror is created by the setting," including "ruins […] crypts, caves, or forests" and "by weather conditions like fog, wind, [and] thunderstorm" (33). We can observe distinct Gothic elements in Tolkien's work, including not only those explained above but also the "old castles with an evil look, as if they had been built by wicked people" seen by Bilbo in the Lone-lands in *The Hobbit* (65). John Garth calls this line "sheer atmosphere – *Gothic* atmosphere," connecting this back to Horace Walpole's original Gothic novel, *The Castle of Otranto* (1794) (2020a, 137). Both Ferdynus and Garth comment on the influence of the past on *The Lord of the Rings*: Ferdynus states that "the past haunts the characters' thoughts and influences their actions" (2016, 37), while Garth similarly says "the distant past still haunts the present […] through the landscape" (2020b).

This "haunting" of the past is explicit in two particularly Gothic scenes in *The Lord of the Rings*: the Paths of the Dead and the Barrow-downs. The Paths of the Dead does not operate much in the Fantastic mode when addressing the experience of Aragorn and Legolas, where the horrific is described relatively plainly and with little ambiguity, but it does when addressing Gimli's experience. When the Grey Company travels, Gimli "was ever hindmost, pursued by a groping horror that seemed always just about to seize him; and a rumour came after him like the shadow-sound of many feet" (*RK*, 'The Passing of the Grey Company,' 787-8). And at the Stone of Erech, when Aragorn blows his horn to call the Dead, "it seemed to those that stood near that they heard a sound of answering horns, as if it was an echo in deep caves far away" (789).

While the Paths of the Dead has much of the Gothic and little of the Fantastic, the Hobbits' experience on the Barrow-downs shows the confluence of both. When they stop near a standing stone at noon for rest before heading out, they find that they have inexplicably fallen asleep in what might be one of the more Fantastic descriptions in *The Lord of the Rings*:

> Riding over hills, and eating their fill, the warm sun and the scent of turf, lying a little too long, stretching out their legs and looking at the sky above their noses; these things are, *perhaps*, enough to explain what happened. However that *may be*: they woke suddenly and uncomfortably from a sleep they had never meant to take. (*FR*, 'Fog on the Barrow-downs', 137)

By giving what would normally be perfectly reasonable explanations for the Hobbits' sleepiness (just as one might blame the turkey for a Thanksgiving nap), Tolkien roots the scene firmly in the normal realm before introducing that uncertainty with a single word, "perhaps," and then we understand that there is reason for doubt.

Just as in the Old Forest, the Hobbits' attempts to make their way through the fog are confounded, but the narrator still introduces uncertainty throughout the passage:

> They *felt as if* a trap was closing about them [...] The valley *seemed* to stretch on endlessly [...] He *could not remember*

having seen any sign [...] so darkness *seemed* to fall round him [...] From some way off, *or so it seemed*, he thought he heard a cry [...] and then it *seemed* faint and far ahead and high above him. (138-9)

And just as with Old Man Willow, once the danger is directly at hand, the ambiguity lessens. For example, in one of the more explicitly horrific images in the book there is no ambiguity when "round the corner a long arm was groping, walking on its fingers towards Sam, who was lying nearest, and towards the hilt of the sword that lay upon him" (141). Again, where before Tolkien built up the tension of the scene through the Fantastic, once the full supernatural is displayed there is no uncertainty, and we emerge fully into the marvelous. The Gothic nature of this scene is further emphasized in Merry's description of his dream-vision, where he takes on the persona of a long-dead warrior killed in a surprise attack by "the Men of Carn Dûm" (143), an example of the past literally haunting the Barrow-downs.

As Ferdynus says, "there is no direct evidence that Tolkien drew inspiration from the Gothic" (2016, 36), but given the line of inspiration from Gothic literature through Victorian Romance (Vaninskaya 2008) and thus to Tolkien, the connections are there even if they are, as Shippey reminds us, not "from one to another" (qtd. in Scull & Hammond 2006, 601). Not only are scenes that explicitly reference the past haunted by it, such as the Barrow-downs and the Paths of the Dead, but so are those that deal specifically with nature; as Treebeard explains, the effects of the Great Darkness of an earlier age are felt even today in places like the Old Forest. We can see that Tolkien learned his craft well, making good use of the Fantastic as a mode for building suspense and tension in his scenes where uncertainty and ambiguity, representing the anxiety of the present, are needed, and we see this use of the Fantastic specifically where Tolkein's work is the most Gothic in feeling. Thus, Todorov's *The Fantastic* may not be directly applicable as an explanation of the genre of modern fantasy, but it can still be used to help us explain how authors accomplish their craft.

Bibliography

Attebery, Brian, *Stories about Stories: Fantasy and the Remaking of Myth*, Kindle (Oxford: Oxford University Press, 2014).
—, 'Structuralism', in *The Cambridge Companion to Fantasy Literature*, ed. by Edward James, Farah Mendlesohn, and Kindle (Cambridge: Cambridge University Press, 2014), pp. 103–14

Cilli, Oronzo, *Tolkien's Library: An Annotated Checklist*, Kindle (Edinburgh: Luna Press Publishing, 2019).

Ferdynus, Katarzyna, 'The Shadow of the Past. *The Lord of the Rings* and the Gothic Novel', *New Horizons in English Studies*, 1.1 (2016), 32–42 <https://doi.org/10.17951/nh.2016.32>

Garth, John, *The Worlds of J.R.R. Tolkien: The Places That Inspired Middle-earth,* (Princeton: Princeton University Press, 2020a).
—, 'Week 11 Lecture 1: The Worlds of J.R.R. Tolkien' (Signum University, 2020b).

Haggard, H. Rider, *She* (London: Longmans, 1887; repr. in *H. Rider Haggard: Collected Novels*, Secaucus, New York: Castle, 1987).

MacDonald, George, *Lilith: A Romance,* (London: Chatto & Windus, 1895; repr. Grand Rapids, Michigan: Wm B Eardman's, 2000).

Morris, William, *The Wood Beyond the World*, Pocket Edition (London: Longmans, Green and Co., 1913; repr. Project Gutenberg) <http://www.gutenberg.org/files/3055/3055-h/3055-h.htm> [accessed 16 November 2020]

Scull, Christina, and Wayne G. Hammond, *The J.R.R. Tolkien Companion & Guide: Reader's Guide,* (Boston: Houghton Mifflin Company, 2006).

Todorov, Tzvetan, *The Fantastic: A Structural Approach to a Literary Genre*, trans. by Richard Howard (Ithaca, New York: Cornell University Press, 1975).

Tolkien, J.R.R., *The Annotated Hobbit*, Revised (Boston: Houghton Mifflin Company, 2002).
—, *The Lord of the Rings*, 50th Anniversary (Boston: Houghton Mifflin Company, 2004).

Vaninskaya, Anna, 'The Late-Victorian Romance Revival: A Generic Excursus', *English Literature in Transition*, 1880-1920, 51.1 (2008), 57–79 <https://doi.org/10.2487/elt.51.1(2008)0015>

Wolfshohl, Clarence, 'William Morris's *The Wood Beyond The World*: The Victorian World vs. The Mythic Eternities', *Mythlore: A Journal of J.R.R. Tolkien, C.S. Lewis, Charles Williams, and Mythopoeic Literature*, 6.3 (1979) <https://dc.swosu.edu/mythlore/vol6/iss3/10>

About the contributors

Mahdî Brecq is a French scandinavist. He works on *riddarasögur*, which are Old Norse adaptations of Old French, Latin and German texts. He is currently preparing the translation of several Icelandic sagas, as well as an anthology of early Germanic poetry focusing on the theme of heroism. He has written several articles on Tolkien's work and the *res germanica*. He has co-translated from German Rudolf Simek's book *Middle-earth: Tolkien and the Germanic-Scandinavian mythology* into French (2019). Finally, he is preparing a collection of studies on Tolkien's work and the Germanic tradition.

Dr. Kristine Larsen has been an astronomy professor at Central Connecticut State University since 1989. Her teaching and research focus on the intersections between science and society, including science and popular culture (especially science in the works of J.R.R. Tolkien) and the history of science. She is the author of the books *Stephen Hawking: A Biography*, *Cosmology 101*, *The Women Who Popularized Geology in the 19th Century*, *Particle Panic!* and *Science, Technology and Magic in The Witcher* (February 2023).

Nick Groom is Professor of Literature in English at the University of Macau, having previously held positions at the universities of Bristol, Stanford, Chicago, and Exeter. He specializes on both the Gothic and Tolkien, and among his books are *The Gothic* (Oxford University Press, 2012) and *The Vampire* (Yale University Press, 2018, 2020); editions of the

Gothic novels *The Castle of Otranto*, *The Monk*, *The Italian*, and *Frankenstein* (all Oxford University Press); and *Twenty-First-Century Tolkien: What Middle-Earth Means To Us Today* (Atlantic, 2022, 2023), which was runner-up for The Tolkien Society Best Book Award 2023.

Sofia Skeva is a postgraduate student in English and American Studies at Aristotle University of Thessaloniki. She holds a BA in English Language and Literature from Aristotle University, and her research interests include (children's) fantasy literature, J.R.R. Tolkien, medievalism, and Gothic literature as well as contemporary American studies (graphic novels, cinema, and popular culture). Her ongoing MA dissertation focuses on post-war British children's portal-quest fantasy literature and postcolonial ecocriticism, while her previous papers explore intersections between fantasy literature and questions of home and (national) identity, Tolkien and adaptation theory, the Gothic double etc. She is an accredited English Language teacher and illustrator.

Michael Dunn is a research associate at the Käte Hamburger Centre for Apocalyptic and Post-Apocalyptic Studies (CAPAS), Heidelberg University where he works in publication management. He is currently a PhD candidate at Heidelberg University working on the framing of ecological apocalypses in modern classic literature. His research interests focus on climate culpability and justice, the ecologically uncanny, literary vampires, and earthly ends.

Journee Cotton is a third year PhD candidate at the University of Exeter studying English. She obtained bachelor degrees from Lubbock Christian University in English focusing in Literature and Humanities focusing in Pre-law and a master's degree in English Literature focusing on the Victorian and Romantic periods at the University of Bristol. She works at the University of Exeter as a Postgraduate Teaching Assistant, an editor for *PJMH: The Postgraduate Journal of Medical Humanities*, and a peer reviewer for *Exclamat!on: An Interdisciplinary Journal*. Her current field of study uses Environmental Bioethics as a framework for the literature of J.R.R. Tolkien. She is interested in Bioethics, Ecology, and body studies.

D.A.K. (Duane) Watson is an instructor at Llano High School in Llano, Texas, teaching English Composition, Economics, Government, and Audio/Visual Art and Technology. He is also a graduate student at Signum University, focusing on imaginative literature, and holds an M.A. in English from National University (La Jolla, California) and an M.Ed. in Curriculum and Instruction from Concordia University - Nebraska. He resides in the Texas Hill Country with his wife, Jen, and their five cats.

Milton Keynes UK
Ingram Content Group UK Ltd.
UKHW030205200324
439698UK00021B/955

9 781915 556370